Praise for *The Bible Is Not Enough*

The rise of Christian nationalism has exposed how our imagination as Americans has been shaped by stories of conflict and conquest: might makes right. But what if our patterns of life were shaped instead by the whole of Scripture? What if we confronted evil with peaceable means to make peace? Scot McKnight's insightful book takes us into the heart of God's agenda in Scripture as it propels us along the path of living out a peaceful imagination.

—**Joel B. Green,** senior professor of
New Testament Interpretation,
Fuller Theological Seminary

Scot McKnight is gentle, but he insists on peace as a Christian essential. Having baptized us in the ocean of the Bible's peace message, he raises us to a peaceful imagination that transcends narrow proof-texting. McKnight's pressing logic, gracious disposition, and passionate advocacy place us "aspiring" pacifists under gospel conviction.

—**Greg Carey,** professor of New Testament,
Lancaster Theological Seminary

McKnight teases out a vision from Scripture in which the peace of the world to come is breaking through in the present, and one which we are called to join. It is a world in which the peace of God brings neighbors and nations together in the peace of Christ. And it's the kind of world I want for all Christians to take part in.

A theological missive against White Christian nationalism and the ways that Christians of all political parties have sanitized the killing of their enemies. *The Bible Is Not Enough* is a wake-up call—an invitation for the church to expand its theological imagination and to improvise God's disruption of political violence through Jesus's way of peace.

THE
BIBLE
IS
NOT ENOUGH

THE
BIBLE
IS
NOT ENOUGH

Imagination
and Making Peace
in the
Modern World

SCOT
MCKNIGHT

Fortress Press
Minneapolis

THE BIBLE IS NOT ENOUGH
Imagination and Making Peace in the Modern World

Library of Congress Control Number: 2023933162 (print)

Cover image: Full frame shot of abstract background - stock photo ©Chris
Stringfellow / 500px | Getty Images
Cover design: Kristin Miller

Print ISBN: 978-1-5064-8804-2
eBook ISBN: 978-1-5064-8805-9

Printed in China.

CONTENTS

1

POVERTY OF IMAGINATION

AMERICA'S CHRISTIAN NATIONALISM is not arising from America's fringe. Seventy percent of white evangelicals think the US Constitution is divinely inspired. Seventy percent. The same demographic thinks violence is fine for us but not for them.[1] And that demographic struts around claiming to be the most faithful Christians in the world. Their reality is itself dystopian.

Official military leaders now justify death, killing, murder, and war as "humane" and are seeking an illusive, yet unattainable, middle ground between obliteration and peace, proposing "humane" war, weapons, and policies. The story of the humane war narrative has now been told.[2] The thesis, rooted in a study of wars, war theory, and war theorists, is that "in our time, swords have not been beaten into plowshares" but instead their swords have been melted down for drones. And drones, official military personnel now claim, are increasingly "the cleanest mode of war ever conceived," and they regard this as a "clear choice to make war more humane." We "Americans are the ones who have invented a form of war righteously pursued as superior precisely for being more humane." But war, which is a quest for domination, justifies "humane" war only by making it endless. America, led far too often by those claiming to be Christians, has turned in one century from the world's peacemaker to a humane warmonger. The war-torn world demands a Christian imagination that has the powers of improvisation—not an imagination marked by self-serving justifications. We have a poverty of imagination.

Donald Trump stretched this new so-called humane war to the next level and beyond. But Bill Clinton and the second Bush were the architects of the humane war strategy, and this was perfected by Barack Obama, who has been imitated by Biden. Universal surveillance has been combined with drone-targeted missiles legitimated by their humane-ness and lack of "collateral damage." Why do more Christians not recognize what war experts know, namely, that "we fight war crimes but have forgotten the crime of war"?

> *KABUL/WASHINGTON, Aug 2 (Reuters) –*
> *The United States killed al Qaeda leader Ayman al-Zawahiri with a drone missile while he stood on a balcony at his home in Kabul, U.S. officials said, the biggest blow to the militants since Osama bin Laden was shot dead more than a decade ago.*
>
> *Afghanistan's Taliban government has not confirmed the death of Zawahiri, an Egyptian surgeon who had a $25 million bounty on his head and helped to coordinate the Sept. 11, 2001, attacks on the United States that killed nearly 3,000 people.*

U.S. officials, speaking on the condition of anonymity, said Zawahiri was killed when he came out on the balcony of his safe house in the Afghan capital at 6:18 a.m. (0148 GMT) on Sunday and was hit by Hellfire missiles from a U.S. drone.

"Now justice has been delivered, and this terrorist leader is no more," U.S. President Joe Biden said on Monday.

Biden said he authorized the strike after months of planning and that no civilians or family members were killed.[3]

The USA's official explanation, as given by Secretary of State Anthony Blinken, reads,

President Biden last year committed to the American people that, following the withdrawal of U.S. forces, the United States would continue to protect our country and act against terrorist threats emanating from Afghanistan. The President made clear that we would not hesitate to protect the Homeland. With the operation that delivered justice to Ayman al-Zawahiri, the leader of al Qa'ida, we have made good on that commitment and we will continue to do so in the face of any future threats. We were able to do so in this instance—and will be positioned to do so going forward—as a result of

> *the skill and professionalism of our intelligence and*
> *counterterrorism community colleagues, for whom*
> *the President and I are deeply grateful.*[4]

These new sponge-covered acts of war are then whitewashed in an attempt to humanize war. Anything can be morally justified if the dominant power's rhetorical ploy transforms acts of war into a moral good. War is violence, war is the crime.

Violence runs deep in America's culture. America at war is a part of its identity. Critics of the Right diminish the significance of the Christian nationalist movement that shook the country on January 6, 2021. One dare not. A second arising could be in the offing. Violence shifts from one dimension of culture to another, from war to gun possession to ordinary citizens packing heat to more humane forms of the death penalty to police violence and to military torture.[5]

There is no balance midway between war and peace. Either you take up your sword, or you renounce war, melt swords into garden tools, and resist violence as a dissident. One holds a weapon or a white flag. Not both. "Humane" weapons remain the tool of the warrior, and pride in a half-mast white flag remains complicit in war. Attempts to balance war and peace betray the power of a peace-reading of the Bible. A Christian theology of peace points its fingers at humane war theory. There is no such thing as a humane war. Gluing "humane" to "war" echoes Orwell's *1984*[6] and apartheid rhetoric—like every empire that has ever existed. War cannot coexist with the humane because war is inhumane.

Peace through strength, however diplomatic, remains war and bloodshed chased down by more violence. Peace through strength, even if said in the kind voice of a movie-star president, is empire ideology. Tacitus once described Rome's military subjugation as "They make a desolation and call it peace."[7] Just war theory is just the Christian empire's attempt to cushion war, even if Christians adhere to the possibility of a just war.[8] Or to some version of Christian realism,[9] which has not produced even one just war, in spite of millions of Christians being engaged in thousands of wars and skirmishes.

One can find political labels for activists of our day. For instance, one might make use of Jonathan Swift's Lilliputians or Yahoos or Houyhnhnms, update them by adding a tattoo or two, and play the game of identification. Labels require a starting point. A peaceful approach begins outside these political labels. One can't start with the Declaration of Independence, the Articles of Confederation, or the US Constitution and get to the peaceful imagination. One must begin elsewhere. It takes no imagination to wage a just or humane war. Both slaughter other humans in the quest for domination under the flag of peace. New imagination requires new beginnings.

The Bible offers some raw materials of a new beginning. But the Bible itself has been become another tool of the "humane." The audaciousness of the Bible has been tamed—tamed, and then co-opted. All too often the Bible is weighed against itself, allowing extreme to mitigate extreme. But that is not how the Bible worked or works. The Bible takes a stand by pressing for one end of the extreme, sometimes even pushing the other end off stage. The Bible did so because the times called for it. The Bible imagines a peaceful world and then insists upon improvisation to realize that peace.

Peace Is Not a Preference

A sketch of the meaning of the term *peace* in the New Testament reveals that God is a God of peace, the message is a gospel of peace, the gospel makes peace with God, and thus believers are to pursue peace among themselves and with others. Paul greets his churches with peace and Paul reminds the Corinthians—with whom he had at least a strained relationship—that the Christian calling is to live in peace. One of the most important visions of the early Christians is found in Ephesians 2, when Paul says Christ is himself the peace that unites gentiles with Jews. That theme expands to cosmic peace in another letter of Paul's, the one to the Colossians.[10] Peace needs to be pressed into action because war and peace cannot themselves be the simultaneous callings of those who follow the way of Jesus. One can't mitigate peace with war and contend for following the teachings of the New Testament.

Peace is not a preference for Christians. Peace is the necessity, the prophetic burden. War must turn from inevitable to the intolerable.[11] The idealistic arc of the universe toward justice will never curve downward without the protestations of those who see through the rhetoric to the reality. Politicians won't bend the arc.

> *The deepest blame for the perpetuation of endless war fell on Obama himself. He established a working relationship with a public that allowed itself to be convinced that his policies of endless and humane war, though not exactly what they had signed up for, were morally wholesome. This effect depended utterly on Obama's rhetorical genius.*[12]

Let it be said for those who want to point to the other side in Congress that finger pointing is entirely accurate. Obama carried on what was there, and none can claim surprise that Trump escalated it. Trump "left no doubt about his opinion of humane war. Trump's statements involved worse than callous disregard for suffering in conflict; he actively praised brutality." Trump believed "torture works,"[13] and he was a fan of the $64 million Reaper drone. The solution can't be found on either side of Congress. The history of our politics devolves to where we are, and it fails to aspire to where we need to be. The so-called Christian America tells a story of the history of war because of the poverty of imagination.

There is an option. Dissidents resisting the crime of war can choose to improvise a peaceful imagination. Such improvisation can be imagined because of the Bible's peace vision, but a peaceful imagination[14] must go beyond the Bible. Such a practice requires an imagination that roots itself in the Bible but improvises a peace vision to a kingdom end.[15] The goal is not a new social policy to replace or augment old ones, but a destabilizing of current policies and their replacement with a peaceful imagination.

Most people label a peaceful imagination as "pacifist," as if that was a weak or dirty word. But one must clarify immediately that pacifism does not mean pacifistic or inactive. Rather, a peaceful imagination is active in nonviolent resistance.[16] There is no need to apologize for the term *pacifism* or to defend the view that it is activist, nonviolent resistance. The so-called temple tantrum of Jesus proves a peaceful imagination can be improvised in nonviolent disruption.[17] A peaceful imagination is social disruption.

2

PROPHETIC IMAGINATION

THE PROPHETS OF the Bible cast powerful images of the future. Their eschatology is an imagination, and their images require an imagination to understand. The literalist interpreters burble on and on about international events and moments, fashioning each image of the prophets into a timeline of real events, in real history, in a real future. Literalism has no imagination. Not only do literalists fail to catch the vision the prophetic imagination offers, their fixation to fit the prophetic word to some modern event or person or nation has proven wrong every time. One could hope one of their own would stand up and announce they've been wrong all along and it's time to abandon the literalistic reading of the Bible's prophets. Such interpretations lack the imagination of the prophet, and so they blunt the power of a Spirit-prompted improvisation.

Prophets of the biblical tradition (Isaiah, Daniel, Jesus, John the seer) operate with a theopoetic and theopolitical scenario of what is about to happen, graphic in description, and then cast a foreground with images evoking an imagined future. And they do so as if the next event would be immediately followed by the end of history. The critics' obsession with proving that the prophets got it wrong, because the end of history didn't arrive, is hung up on the same literalism as the fundamentalists. Prophetic language is dramatic, fictive, rhetorically shaped imagination meant to provoke a response of repentance, justice, and peace. Imagination stimulating improvisation. Not predictions demanding closer readings of newspapers or websites.

Prophets stimulate a peaceful imagination.[1] To enter their imaginations requires an aesthetic, if not an ecstatic, sensibility as their images turn words into vision as music turns words into sound. The prophet's peaceful imagination is not a flight of fancy, it is not fantasy or marvel or even fiction as we might know it. The prophet is inspired by the prophetic Spirit to speak a word from God to the people, and so cast a vision for the transformation of society. Yet, a prophetic imagination expresses and appeals to the hope of the oppressed, the exiled, the marginalized. A peaceful imagination is a counterfactual of the present world. Imagination is required for what transcends the mundane, and few can doubt the need for transcendence when it comes to peace. Imagination is faith and, when a person steps in the direction of peace out of the mundane, faith becomes action. As such, the peaceful imagination is an act of resistance and becomes the natural language of dissidents.[2] The words of the prophets are not so much prediction as imagination, but it is the kind of faith-inspired imagination that stimulates humans to live into that imagined, alternative world—or at least enter it. The prophet's language is like the wardrobe into Narnia.[3]

Israel's Prophets

In exile the prophet Isaiah's imagination awakens to offer to the exiles a return home. The return to a renewed life in the land is buoyed up by an imagination of peace (and justice and holiness). This vision is rooted in God's faithfulness to the covenant promises when God's glory will be seen by all the nations (Isa 49–55). *Shalom* is an "iridescent word" and can mean prosperity, safety, salvation, personal and interpersonal peacefulness, blessing, well-being, healing and health, moral goodness and holiness, wholeness, and rest.[4] As an imaginative vision, shalom describes a nation, a people, a temple, and an economy serving God and one another. It describes a spirituality of society living out words, thoughts, and deeds in the way of peace.

The stunning images in Isaiah and Micah get us started.

> *He shall judge between the nations,*
> *and shall arbitrate for many peoples;*
> *they shall beat their swords into plowshares,*
> *and their spears into pruning hooks;*
> *nation shall not lift up sword against nation,*
> *neither shall they learn war any more.*
>
> *He shall judge between many peoples,*
> *and shall arbitrate between strong nations*
> *far away;*

> *they shall beat their swords into plowshares,*
> *and their spears into pruning hooks;*
> *nation shall not lift up sword against nation,*
> *neither shall they learn war any more.*[5]

Here we see a kingdom kind of vision in which all *war will cease* because those who experience that kind of world will press swords to the anvil and repurpose them as farm implements. Isaiah's improvised future included a messianic figure who would be the "Prince of Peace," and the peaceful world would be "endless." Peace is the "effect of righteousness" and the people "will abide in a peaceful habitation, in secure dwellings, and in quiet resting places."

Here are some of Isaiah's words filled with imagination, words fertilized by divine discipline, words about the people's imminent return to Zion *with utter joy*:

> *So the ransomed of the LORD shall return,*
> *and come to Zion with singing;*
> *everlasting joy shall be upon their heads;*
> *they shall obtain joy and gladness,*
> *and sorrow and sighing shall flee away.*[6]

The prophet's imagination strikes the notes of *beauty because the liberation of the exiles means their God has begun to reign.* Those waiting and watching for the return of Yahweh to Zion, the holy hill, will spot the exiles coming, and what they will announce ties together peace, gospel, salvation, and God's kingdom.

> *How beautiful upon the mountains*
> *are the feet of the messenger who announces*
> *peace,*
> *who brings good news,*
> *who announces salvation,*
> *who says to Zion, "Your God reigns."*
> *Listen! Your sentinels lift up their voices,*
> *together they sing for joy;*
> *for in plain sight they see*
> *the return of the LORD to Zion.*

So *numerous* will the inhabitants of the land be, and so *abundant* their produce, and so *expansive* their borders, that they will need to build *additions* to their homes as they *push their captors out of the land*:

> *Enlarge your tent space,*
> *people must stretch your dwelling curtains,*
> *don't hold back. . . .*
> *Your offspring will dispossess the nations.*

God's promise to them is *a covenant of peace*, one that promises *a society at rest* in the protection of God:

> *. . . and my covenant of peace shall be removed.*

> *All your children will be Yahweh's disciples;*
>   *great will be your children's* well-being.

They will depart from Babylon, and they shall arrive home in Jerusalem:

> *For you shall go out* in joy,
>   *and be led back* in peace.

The images in Isaiah's vision of peace explode with joy and flourishing in the land because the people of God are liberated from bondage to enter into the safe spaces of redemption. The people will all be healed. The imaginative word for the people is that "I will appoint Peace as your overseer and Righteousness as your taskmaster." Before the prophet signs off he explicates what peace looks like in the land:

> *I will extend prosperity to her like a river,*
>   *and the wealth of the nations like an*
>   *overflowing stream;*
> *and you shall nurse and be carried on her arm,*
>   *and dandled on her knees.*
> *As a mother comforts her child,*
>   *so I will comfort you;*
>   *you shall be comforted in Jerusalem.*
> *You shall see, and your heart shall rejoice;*
>   *your bodies shall flourish like the grass;*

> *and it shall be known that the hand of the*
>   *LORD is with his servants,*
>   *and his indignation is against his enemies.*

Other prophets operate with the same imagination, one fueled at times by Isaiah. Jeremiah promises no sword and no famine because peace and prosperity will come. One of the more popular lines from Jeremiah known to many is from chapter 29, but the translations lead some to miss the word *peace*, which has been emphasized here:

> *But seek the* peace *of the city where I have sent you into exile, and pray to the LORD on its behalf, for in its* peace *you will find your* peace. *(altered; NRSV has "welfare")*

Ezekiel's covenant of peace imagines no more "wild animals," an "everlasting covenant," an increase in numbers, and God's "sanctuary among them forevermore." One of the richest images of peace in the prophets of Israel comes from Zechariah, who imagines a land producing in abundance, and a people observing the laws of God.

> *For there shall be a sowing of peace; the vine shall yield its fruit, the ground shall give its produce, and the skies shall give their dew; and I will cause the remnant of this people to possess all these things.*

> *These are the things that you shall do: Speak the*
> *truth to one another, render in your gates judgments*
> *that are true and make for peace, do not devise evil*
> *in your hearts against one another, and love no*
> *false oath; for all these are things that I hate, says*
> *the LORD.*

So the psalmist, from another time, offers the prayer of peace:

> *Pray for the peace of Jerusalem:*
>   *"May they prosper who love you.*
> *Peace be within your walls,*
>   *and security within your towers."*
> *For the sake of my relatives and friends*
>   *I will say, "Peace be within you."*

Above we said peace is "iridescent" among the prophets. Indeed, it is. And multifaceted and material and earthly and interpersonal and ecological and environmental. It takes an imagination courageous enough to improvise to read these prophets and walk out from Narnia into the real world and live such a peace.

Peace is not a preference. It is the Christian's calling.

The New Testament's Peaceful Imagination

Luke turns the wheel for the peaceful imagination before the other evangelists. John the Baptist's father was a priest, and his song, the Benedictus, was the song of a prophet. Every line in this song echoes the peace vision of ancient Israel's prophets:

> *Then his father Zechariah was filled with the*
> *Holy Spirit and spoke this prophecy:*
>
> *Blessed be the Lord God of Israel,*
>   *for he has looked favorably on his people*
>   *and redeemed them.*
> *He has raised up a mighty savior for us*
>   *in the house of his servant David,*
> *as he spoke through the mouth of his holy*
>   *prophets from of old,*
>   *that we would be saved from our enemies*
>   *and from the hand of all who hate us.*
> *Thus he has shown the mercy promised to our*
>   *ancestors,*
>   *and has remembered his holy covenant,*
> *the oath that he swore to our ancestor Abraham,*
>   *to grant us that we, being rescued from the*
>   *hands of our enemies,*
> *might serve him without fear, in holiness and*
>   *righteousness*
>   *before him all our days.*
> *And you, child, will be called the prophet of*
>   *the Most High;*
>   *for you will go before the Lord to prepare*
>   *his ways,*

> to give knowledge of salvation to his people
>   by the forgiveness of their sins.
> By the tender mercy of our God,
>   the dawn from on high will break upon us,
> to give light to those who sit in darkness and
>   in the shadow of death,
>   to guide our feet into the way of peace.
>   (Luke 1:67–79)

Notice where the song ends. All the redemptive work of God that will occur through Zechariah's son and their relative (Jesus!) will lead them, as the exiles were led back, "into the way of peace." Which is why Luke's angels sing the same song of redemption when they say "on earth peace among those whom he favors" (2:14). A peaceful imagination is launched into reality with the advent of Jesus.

Jesus embraced the peaceful imagination of the prophets and expanded it. Here is a brief sketch of his peace statements.[7] Jesus's Beatitudes in Matthew bless various fly-over people, and in one of them he pronounces divine favor on "peacemakers," which means people who do acts that make for peace. These are the ones who will be called the children of God. His words cut against the grain of the zealous defense of nation, law, temple, and people. Though the term *peace* does not show up often in Luke, it is worth noting this summary statement: the agents of Jesus offer a message of peace resting upon a home as those who receive them are termed "sons of peace." Peace's importance crops up again as Jesus laments over the city, saying, "If you, even you, had only recognized on this day the things that make for peace!" Peace takes on its inner sense in John's Gospel, the kind of peace that can endure opposition.[8]

One does not have to dig deep into Jewish texts of the day to know that Jesus's generation arose and passed on its inheritances in a world surrounded by violence in many forms. To read Josephus's *Jewish War* or 1–2 Maccabees, or the visions and expectations of those dwelling at Qumran, or to ponder stories of the various zealot movements of that day is to know that Jesus's word *peace* was a loud drumbeat overwhelmed by the clashing sword sounds of his day.[9]

A stinger appears in Peter's sermon in Cornelius's household when he summarizes Jesus's own gospel preaching in these words in the tenth chapter: "You know the message he sent to the people of Israel, preaching peace by Jesus Christ—he is Lord of all," and he says it was "that message" that was "spread throughout Judea" from Galilee south once John's baptism was proclaimed. When Peter summarizes the gospel *actions* of Jesus, he turns to the "doing good" (benefactions) and "healing" those "oppressed by the devil" (Acts 10:36–38). Jesus preached a peace gospel that brought holistic redemption, and this is a vision that can set one's imagination on fire for various forms of improvisation in our day as it did in the first century.

Paul himself speaks of the "kingdom of God" only rarely, but in a noticeable instance in Romans he writes that the kingdom is "not food and drink but righteousness and peace and joy in the Holy Spirit."[10] His God is the "God of peace" who will usher in final peace by crushing "Satan under" the feet of the Roman believers. He seems to return to the theme of Peter's sermon mentioned just above when he writes of the "gospel of peace."

James's brief word about peace near the end of chapter 3 connects two terms drawn from the peaceful imagination of the prophets (peace and righteousness) as he echoes, as he often does, the words of Jesus. He says, "A harvest of righteousness is sown in peace for those who make peace" (Jas 3:18). One has to embrace peace if one wants to improvise policies of peace with a peaceful imagination.

John the Seer

Revelation is taking some deserved hits today for its graphic violence, but the criticisms at times are based on a reading as literalistic as the literalists they deride. It takes an imagination, if not more, to comprehend the vision of peace in this book. The scope of its vision is clear enough: for New Jerusalem to be established, the Lamb must defeat the agents of the Dragon and its wild things. The salient features of John's imagining of a final, lasting peace from the final two chapters of Revelation provide an adequate reprise of the book's vision for peace.

God will dwell with the people of New Jerusalem to renew the covenant relationship; grief and death will end because they belong to the "first things"; everything will be new because it will exclude those who resist the ways of God. As with Ezekiel, an angel transports John to a mountain so he can see a glorious, bejeweled New Jerusalem. Unlike Ezekiel, there is "no temple" because "its temple is the Lord God Almighty and the Lamb." So effulgent is the glory of God that there is "no need of sun or moon." Peace means all "nations will walk by its light, and the kings of the earth" will return what they have accumulated by exploitation from others and "bring their glory" to New Jerusalem. So safe is the city that "its gates will never be shut" (Rev 21:22–25).

John's imagining of the city of peace continues. The Edenic river of life flows into the city to water the tree of life on either side, and the leaves of that tree "are for the healing of the nations" (Rev 22:22). God's people, who have God's name tattooed to their heads, will worship God.

Peace

Among the Bible's prophets peace is so broad one must contend that peace involves salvation and liberation, justice and material blessing, interpersonal harmony and health and economic justice . . . one could go on. Peace is an imagined reality that inspires a person to improvise, in her specific situation and location, a way of life that counters the way of violence and death. The reason we are stuck in the "humane" war and white Christian nationalism is in part because those who claim most to follow Jesus lack a peaceful imagination that can shake systemic structures of violence and war to the ground.

But for a Christian to form such an imagination, a renewed commitment must be made to Jesus's kingdom, which in turn gives rise to an improvisation of peace.

3

KINGDOM IMAGINATION

AN UNIMPEACHABLE DIMENSION of the earliest Christian movement and its record in the New Testament is that with Jesus something happened, and that something was new. The theme is so pervasive one could go on for pages listing passages. Jesus's own term for that something new is *kingdom*. The ethical vision for the Christian today, including a response to "humane" war tactics, should be rooted first in Jesus's kingdom imagination and in the new reality of him as Lord.[1] Only after studying Jesus do we enter the implications of Pauline ethics or ponder later developments in the Christian ethical tradition. A disciplined framework for a Christian ethic begins with Jesus.

Something New

Jesus reached back into the prophetic vision and made it his own. Jesus began with Isaiah 61:1–3. Isaiah's words formed his vision, mission, and action. In Luke's Gospel Jesus opens his public mission in his hometown synagogue quoting an Isaiah text and then declaring Isaiah's fulfillment.

> *When he came to Nazareth, where he had been brought up, he went to the synagogue on the sabbath day, as was his custom. He stood up to read, and the scroll of the prophet Isaiah was given to him. He unrolled the scroll and found the place where it was written:*
>
> > *"The Spirit of the Lord is upon me,*
> >   *because he has anointed me*
> >   *to bring good news to the poor.*
> > *He has sent me to proclaim release to the*
> >   *captives*
> >   *and recovery of sight to the blind,*
> >   *to let the oppressed go free,*
> > *to proclaim the year of the Lord's favor."*
>
> *And he rolled up the scroll, gave it back to the attendant, and sat down. The eyes of all in the synagogue were fixed on him. Then he began to say to them, "Today this scripture has been fulfilled in your hearing." (4:16–21)*

Key ingredients in Jesus's kingdom mission appear in this short passage: Isaiah, Spirit, the gospel, the poor, liberation, and Jubilee.

Once the stage is set in Matthew's Sermon on the Mount, Jesus turns toward the relationship of his teachings to the law of Moses. Perhaps critics of Jesus had asked if he was still an observant Jew, or perhaps others accused him of setting the whole law aside. Whatever their questions or accusations, Jesus seems to be responding with a denial: "Do not think that I have come to abolish the law or the prophets" (5:17). Rather, Jesus says, he has come "to fulfill." That term (*plēroō*) carries in its satchel respect for both the law and the prophets as well as a sense that something new is happening. That term *fulfill* is Matthew's favorite term for pinning something new to Jesus.[2] *History has come to a turning point, to a resolution in Jesus,*[3] which means his teachings now govern those who follow him. He comes off as a rabbi with a distinctive brand of teaching. Disciples following Jesus will have a righteousness that greatly exceeds the standard set by the scribes and Pharisees.

When the crowds asked Jesus about John the Baptist he made this observation: "From the days of John the Baptist until now the kingdom of heaven has suffered violence, and the violent take it by force." That saying shows up slightly differently with, "The law and the prophets were in effect until John came; since then the good news of the kingdom of God is proclaimed, and everyone tries to enter it by force."[4] Luke says "the law and the prophets" were "until" or "as far as" John.[5] The text does not say the law is suspended or abolished. Instead, the words of Jesus assert an *undeniable chapter division in Israel's story*. Until the law and the prophets—but after the law and prophets comes "the kingdom of God." Jesus preaches the kingdom "and everyone tries to enter it." Something new is at work.

This something new theme becomes *personal* in the next chapter of Matthew's Gospel. The followers of Jesus were accused of working on the Sabbath for plucking heads of wheat from the stalks. Jesus reminds them that David did much the same in the temple, and then he utters two sayings that speak to the newness theme. When he says "something greater than the temple is here" (12:6), Jesus at least believes something greater has been launched. To make it personal, Jesus quasi-identifies himself with that something greater when he says, "The Son of Man is lord of the sabbath" (12:8). The title Son of Man could mean little more than a human, that is, "a son of man." But one good look at the expression "lord of the sabbath" raises the level of the claim. Son of Man evokes the special representative figure who will alter history. We read about the Son of Man in Daniel 7.[6] Jesus himself is the something new at work in this passage.

The newness theme pervades. In the last week, at the Last Supper, Jesus *does something new with Passover.*[7] The earliest account of the Last Supper, found in 1 Corinthians 11:23–26, takes us back into the second decade after Jesus, and at that point it is beyond clear that Jesus *identified his body and his blood with the bread and the wine.* The implications, not to mention the chutzpah, stagger the unsuspecting. Here is a Jewish man in the first century somehow connecting himself—body and blood—with God's covenant with Israel. The something new shifts from the personal to covenant redemption for those eating and drinking.[8] The famous sayings in John's Gospel about eating and drinking "me" only sharpen the sense of the Last Supper.[9] In eating and drinking at the Last Supper, the participant embodies what it means to eat and drink "me" we read about in John's Gospel.[10]

This something new in Christ moves beyond the personal to transform how the Christian approaches and responds to military conflicts, the so-called humane developments in war, white Christian nationalism, torture, and the death penalty. A kingdom imagination includes peace in the something new with Jesus: *to the degree the kingdom has been inaugurated, to that same degree its vision of peace can be realized in this life.* To live now as if the kingdom was not launched denies Jesus's teachings. The church's tragedy about peace is its failure to embody a lived theology of the kingdom.

A Christian approach to living ethically in our world begins with Jesus, but it moves forward to the apostles as well. The something new in the book of Acts, chapter 2, is a momentous event we call Pentecost.[11] Luke presents Pentecost as bringing into reality prophetic words of the prophet Joel about God distributing the Spirit to all—sons and daughters, young men and old men, and slaves. The Spirit imagined by Joel empowers such persons to witness to the resurrection of Jesus as Israel's Messiah and Lord. The onrushing of the Spirit on followers of Jesus leads to a sermon by Peter that calls anyone to repentance and baptism in order to experience both forgiveness and the gift of the Spirit. The pervading presence of the Spirit in Acts is then something new.

The apostle Paul's newness theme is also a Spirit newness, namely, that "the Spirit at work in us *transcends human ability* and *transforms human inability*."[12] A vortex of radical newness occurs when Paul mixes into the vision of something new the terms *Spirit*, *grace*, *faith*, and *Christ*. This vortex writes a new chapter into history. Paul tells the Galatians that until "faith came" "we" were "imprisoned and guarded under the law." The law of Moses was designed by God to last only "until Christ came," and now that he has come "we" are "no longer under a disciplinarian."[13] Paul believes something dramatic, even apocalyptic, happened in Christ and in the gift of the Spirit. The something new leads to a new life.

It is no wonder, then, that the apostle Paul can, even if hyperbolically and in a moment of enthusiasm, express himself in these words: "So if anyone is in Christ, there is a new creation: everything old has passed away; see, everything has become new!"[14]

Perhaps John's words best summarize the theme of something new: "Beloved, I am writing you no new commandment, but an old commandment that you have had from the beginning; the old commandment is the word that you have heard. Yet I am writing you a new commandment that is true in him and in you, because the darkness is passing away and the true light is already shining."[15] New, yet old, yet new.

The thesis then is that the earliest Christians believed something new happened in Jesus. Jesus taught the same.

Jesus and Something New

Jesus teaches something new with the word *kingdom*. The Gospels have statements in which the kingdom is clearly future (consistent eschatology) and others in which the kingdom is in some sense present (realized eschatology).[16] The best answer to the "When is the kingdom arriving?" question is a both-and. The kingdom is both present and future, and the future will be the consummation of the present. Jesus taught a *both now and not yet* understanding of the kingdom.[17]

The When question (future or present? Or both?) often never moves into the "What is the kingdom?" question. The further question, then, is, *If the kingdom is both now and not yet, in what sense is the kingdom present and in what sense is the kingdom future?* The terms used to answer that question come from the Synoptic tradition, and for those who approach questions like the death penalty, Christian nationalism's affirmation of violence, or the "humane" war solution, what Jesus means by the presence of the kingdom offers to Christians a peaceful imagination that can be improvised in our day.

The kingdom is *present* in that Jesus thinks his mission of redemption for his people is the fulfillment of Jewish hope[18] and that he is the agent of launching the kingdom. In other words, Jesus is someone God appointed to herald the gospel of the kingdom, to embody it, and to enact it through what he does. Put in other terms, he's got to be the Messiah.[19] To swear allegiance to Jesus the king, the kingdom launcher, is to ban drone-bombing conquering power. Instead, he presents his kind of empire as an inauspicious, humble presence even as the kingdom's redemption displays power and strength.[20] This newness is profoundly different, then, for how power is wielded. Jesus's kingdom does not conquer all, murder the dissidents, and enslave those who willingly surrender. No, his summons into the kingdom respects agency and will on the part of those who hear his call. Those who follow him are summoned into a radical, kingdom-shaped discipleship.[21] So new is his newness and so radical is discipleship, that Jesus paves the way for a new kind of discipleship when he suffers and dies for his own. Which in turn further defines what discipleship means.[22] Without jumping ahead too quickly, what is present about the kingdom is a king who gives himself for others. This immediately redefines life for those who want to follow Jesus. Those who claim to follow Jesus, the one who gave himself for others, *cannot embrace war and will inevitably embrace a peaceful imagination because discipleship forms them into a life for others.* The kingdom, then, is present in Jesus and around Jesus as a redemptive power that liberates from sin and sickness and systemic injustice by imagining and embodying an alternative life, namely, one of serving so that others may live. His something new in the kingdom requires something more in how one lives.

Jesus's peaceful imagination of the kingdom has its eyes on the future kingdom toward which those on the journey travel. Jesus stands next to all the prophets before him. Each had a vision of the future. Jesus anticipated God fully launching the kingdom in an imminent future that would be like the present but also transcend the present.[23] With the prophets he expected God to begin with a judgment. Jesus said he would administer that judgment and it would put evil to death and bring to life what is good.[24] And, in the final kingdom the followers of Jesus would experience the presence of God the Father and all of God's earthly blessings.[25] Jesus's final kingdom is not some faraway up-in-the-sky spiritual existence where humans would zip on angels' wings and flit from one home to another. For Jesus, as for all the Jewish prophets, the kingdom would be earthy and earthly and Jerusalem centered. It would be a real flesh-and-blood existence after the resurrection. Once again, this kind of earthy vision for the final kingdom reshapes Christian existence in the present as the followers of Jesus seek to embody that future world in the present world. Peace is at the heart of such an earthy, earthly imagination.

Kingdom people have a vision for kingdom living, which begins with a life in community with other kingdom people.[26] For Jesus the kingdom is a sociopolitical reality, a transnational and international reality, and cannot be reduced, as it often has been, to some kind of spiritual, personal, private relationship with God. It is not Western, it is not American. A kingdom, let's get real here, is a people in allegiance to a king!

Kings rule their kingdoms, and they frequently do so by liberating, saving, and rescuing the people. In the Bible's pages this act of liberation has two primary events: the exodus from Egypt and the cross/resurrection of Jesus, not neglecting the empowerment of the Spirit. Over those who have been liberated, the king (God, Jesus) governs. Hence, a people forms the community. And, a king who redeems and rules a people provides for them a law by which to live, and a king establishes a place or location for that people to live. These elements need to be detailed because the kingdom vision of peace that Jesus teaches forms a people into a way of life that ought to challenge the way of Rome and the way of empire today.

Jesus, of course, did not believe the kingdom was *entirely present nor were all the powers of the kingdom launched*, but there was undoubtedly something new. That something new includes the blossoming of a peaceful imagination. But that same something new set in motion an ongoing discernment and improvisation of what it means for kingdom-soaked persons to live in the twenty-first century. And that something new entails that his followers follow him in a way that is something *more*.

A Jesus-soaked peaceful imagination only takes root with a kingdom imagination. It is this imagination that can liberate the people of Jesus from its shackles to violence and death to improvise the way of peace when surrounded by presidents and powers that care more about domination and conquest than goodness and justice. The power of that liberation is unleashed by and in Jesus's kingdom. Those who enter into the kingdom's something new are called to the kingdom's something more.

A kingdom imagination shapes the entirety of discipleship. The something new that happened in Jesus generated a new way of life. What happened with king Jesus—his life, his teachings, his actions, his interactions, his forming of followers, his death, his resurrection, his ascension, his sending of the Spirit—and his impact altered everything for those who chose to follow in his wake. His something new created his something more for his kingdom people.

Righteousness

In Matthew 5:20, Jesus claims to fulfill the law and the prophets while affirming the eternal validity of both. He also contends that loosening the integrity of "one of the least of these commandments" (as he interprets them) will be called "least in the kingdom of heaven." To be "least" is a clever bit of indirection that means exclusion. On the other hand, the one who "does" and "teaches" the law as Jesus interprets the law will be "called great in the kingdom of heaven." Which means inclusion. Jesus's claim of this now-fulfilled law, a vision of how to live that neither dispenses with the law nor leaves it as it is, leads Jesus to *something more* for kingdom people. He claims that his disciples can attain a "righteousness" that "exceeds" the current observance *greatly*.[27] In Jesus's word *greatly* there had to be something observable. Using a word so grandiose as *greatly* does not suggest some subtle little nuance. Jesus counters the standards and behaviors of those in his inner-Jewish observance discussions, the "scribes and Pharisees." He thinks his followers will stand out and above theirs. Righteousness for the scribes and Pharisees points to behaviors consistent with the law of Moses as they interpreted it. Jesus counters their teachings by adhering to the same law but as he interpreted it.[28] To be righteous for Jesus's sparring partners was to follow their interpretations; to be righteous for Jesus's kingdom people was to follow *his* interpretations. That is the difference, the major and perhaps only difference, between Jesus and the Pharisees (and their scribes). That difference is also the something more Jesus expects of kingdom people.

Those who claim to follow him and do not exceed the standards and behaviors of the scribes and Pharisees in an observable manner "will never enter the kingdom of heaven." One cannot unhear the gasps of those listening to Jesus. Jesus believes one must observe his teaching to enter into the kingdom. Something new, something more. That *more* is spelled out with jaw-dropping clarity in the rest of Matthew's fifth chapter: hateful anger is tantamount to murder, desiring a woman other than one's spouse is adultery, divorce permissions are restricted to their original Mosaic grounds, honesty prohibits making oaths and vows, retaliation—humane or not!—contradicts the way of Jesus, and one's enemies are to be turned into neighbors by loving them. It's fair to ask how noticeable the differences were between Jesus's followers then and the scribes and Pharisees, just as it is fair to ask if there are noticeable differences today between those who follow Jesus and those who don't. One difference could easily be detected if those who follow Jesus today would resist "humane" war policies and acts.

Love

Jesus, in a thoroughly Jewish move that calls into question those who frame interpretation and observance differently, makes love central.[29] John's Gospel and 1 John will make love a "new" commandment while simultaneously claiming that love is also an "old" commandment. It is. Two Gospels locate Jesus's words affirming the centrality of loving God and loving others in the final week, but Luke uses that same teaching much earlier in his Gospel. He chose to set up the parable of the Samaritan with Jesus's teaching about loving God and loving others. In these famous passages in the Gospels, we discover a combination of Deuteronomy's love of God, which opened the Shema ("Hear O Israel . . ."), with loving one's neighbor as oneself as found in Leviticus. Love of God and love of others forms the heart of Jesus's interpretation of the law of Moses. That love is the something more of Jesus. At least one implication of Jesus's words about love for current followers of Jesus is that a Christian way of life is love based. Love cannot but guide a follower of Jesus to pursue a peaceful imagination and its modern improvisations.

What may surprise us, in spite of the routine emphasis of love for Jesus, is how rarely peace is mentioned in our talk about Christian ethics.[30] One cannot separate loving God or loving others from pursuing peace.

No better witness of love's centrality for Jesus can be found than what occurs at the end of Matthew's fifth chapter, where Jesus requires his followers to *love their enemies* (5:43–48).[31] *Love* is a word we all can approve, but when we attach "enemies" to it the approval gets some raised eyebrows. What makes this enemy love so radical is that Jesus's something more means turning enemies into neighbors.

Most of us immediately think, after being reminded of Jesus's instruction to love our enemies into neighbors, of who might be our enemies. The humane habits of America's war actions as well as the violence of Christian nationalism contradict what it means to love an enemy, because neither war nor nationalism exists without despising and even hating the other. The scribe who provoked Jesus to teaching about loving God and loving others unmasks himself by asking "Who then is my neighbor?" in a way that suggests less demand, a kind of "To whom do I not have to be neighborly?" In mind for him were contemporary (perceived or real) enemies—like Rome, Samaria, Egypt. Jesus turns around to inform the scribe that anyone on your path is your neighbor, no exceptions granted (Luke 10:25–37).[32] For Jesus there are no enemies, only neighbors and potential neighbors, and his posture creates a peaceful imagination informed by love of God and love of others.

The authors of the Bible did not provide a dictionary of their own terms with the books. And we cannot find what the Bible's authors mean by *love* in English dictionaries, nor does one learn what love is simply by observing humans. A biblical sense of love is best observed in watching God love. God's love is expected of God's people as well. That kind of love, written into the fabric of Israel's own law and stories, is a covenanted, affective committed relationship with another person that involves presence, advocacy, and mutual growth in virtue.

Something new (kingdom) calls for something more (love) so much, that love becomes Jesus's ruling virtue.[33] In all situations at all times.

Thus, Jesus's love of enemy challenges every human in history, not just first-century Galileans or Judeans. Nothing challenges the lack of imagination in contemporary "humane" acts of war, in torture, in the death penalty, and in acts of insurrection in the United States, more than the demand of Jesus upon his followers to love enemies until they become neighbors. When his followers join ranks with the warriors and nationalists they betray Jesus.

The author of the New Testament who uses *love* the most is the apostle Paul,[34] and we are aware that 1 John is—how else to put it—stuck on love. As if he felt compelled to adjust one basic sentence a dozen times. But the prominence of love in Paul and John owes its origins to Jesus's double commandment of love.

Jesus's kingdom, his something new, requires something more of his followers: a righteousness that measures up to his standard of Mosaic observance and a love that reshapes all our behaviors toward others. Both righteousness and love become concrete social reality when Jesus teaches about the cross and then endures the cross for others.

Cross

We need to connect two terms—*kingdom* and *king*.[35] The nature of the kingdom is shaped by the nature of the king, and the earliest Christian story narrates a crucified king. Not a conquering, sword-flashing king. The king of Jesus's kingdom was conquered by the empire's king. The nature of the king shapes the nature of the kingdom. Discipleship to Jesus the king and into his kingdom becomes a cross-shaped life. Jesus's kingdom imagination is improvised by him into a cross-shaped kingdom and a cross-shaped life. Here one finds both the radical edge of Jesus's kingdom vision and a radical reorientation for improvisation in our world today. Here we find an even fuller vision of his something new becoming something more.

The Gospels are biographies,[36] but there's something about the concentration of the Gospels on a passion narrative that forms the something more for those who follow the way of Jesus. The Christian tradition of following Jesus, often called the *imitatio Christi*, is at the heart of the Gospels. Imitation also prompted ancient biographies.[37] One wrote a biography of a person worthy of emulation. However, the pattern of Jesus's life diverged from other patterns of life because Jesus's biographers concentrated their narration on the last week. A last week that narrated his suffering and crucifixion.

The nature of the king shapes the nature of discipleship. Mark's Gospel probably first formulated a something more kingdom discipleship when he put smack-dab in the middle of his Gospel the following words:

> *Then he began to teach them that the Son of Man must undergo great suffering, and be rejected by the elders, the chief priests, and the scribes, and be killed, and after three days rise again. He said all this quite openly. And Peter took him aside and began to rebuke him. But turning and looking at his disciples, he rebuked Peter and said, "Get behind me, Satan! For you are setting your mind not on divine things but on human things." (Mark 8:31–33)*

The nature of Jesus's life then is a life that knows and embraces suffering. That something totally new leads to something totally new in discipleship. Mark continues by spelling out a something more discipleship:

> *He called the crowd with his disciples, and said to them, "If any want to become my followers, let them*

> *deny themselves and take up their cross and follow*
> *me. For those who want to save their life will lose*
> *it, and those who lose their life for my sake, and for*
> *the sake of the gospel, will save it. For what will it*
> *profit them to gain the whole world and forfeit their*
> *life? Indeed, what can they give in return for their*
> *life? Those who are ashamed of me and of my words*
> *in this adulterous and sinful generation, of them the*
> *Son of Man will also be ashamed when he comes in*
> *the glory of his Father with the holy angels." (Mark*
> *8:34–38)*

The connection of Jesus's cross to the disciple's is the ultimate expression of something new creating something more. The way of Jesus becomes the way of the disciple, and since the way of Jesus is a path from the Galilee down and up to Jerusalem onto a cross for others, the way of a disciple is the way of the cross for others. By the way, Luke clarifies that one must take up the cross "daily" (Luke 9:23). Discipleship means self-denial, cross-taking, and following Jesus, and following Jesus is both a physical reality and an inner-spiritual reality that involves commitment, cost, and community with suffering.[38] Luke's Gospel constructs a narrative journey from the Galilee to Jerusalem, and the cross that awaits him in Jerusalem looms over the narrative from Luke 9:51 on. The heart of Luke's Gospel leads a follower of Jesus to the cross, and for those who choose to follow him, to a life that embraces the cross life. (Paul, too, will embrace a cross-shaped life for how church members were to live.[39] We can call this way of life "cruciformity" or "Christoformity."[40])

A peaceful imagination derived from a kingdom imagination leads to a way of life that is reshaped by the cross-shaped life of Jesus. Followers of Jesus today must be willing to ask if "humane" war or aggressive Christian nationalism can ever be squared up with the something more Jesus asks of his followers, then or today.

They can't.

What we need today is a peaceful kingdom imagination with the courage to improvise.

4

IMPROVISATIONAL IMAGINATION

THE NEW TESTAMENT vision for how best to live develops out of the Jewish legal tradition. Contending that Christian morals derive from law may jar some readers, so it will require some explanation. Many, if not most, Christians glue the words *legalism* and *tradition* to the Pharisees and then, knowingly or not, those same Christians slide down the hill of anti-Judaism or insulting the heritages of both Jesus and the apostles. Then Christians begin to denigrate anything connected to law. Law is bad, grace and gospel are good. These all-too-common postures toward the law of Moses have made honest readings of what Jesus is actually doing in Matthew 5 impossible. In Matthew 5 Jesus offered his own interpretation of the law of Moses. He didn't dismiss the law; he contributed to the Jewish legal tradition. Of course he had differences with the scribes and Pharisees but, c'mon friends, who didn't? They differed with one another, and debating it out gave them life and joy.

Jesus proposed in Matthew 5 a kingdom-based improvisation of the law of Moses. The implication for us is that we can learn from Jesus how we, today and tomorrow, can improvise both the law and the teachings of Jesus for our world.

Improvisation is how a legal tradition works. Ask any lawyer. It requires a kingdom imagination to improvise kingdom teachings well.

Law Develops

We have today in the United States legal theories that are often called "originalism" or "constitutionalism," practiced in various ways by former Supreme Court Justice Antonin Scalia and by current Justice Clarence Thomas.[1] In this approach to law the original intent and original context form the basis of legal rulings. So, to apply originalism to the Bible, take some Jewish or early Christian writings, say, what Moses said in Deuteronomy or what Jesus said in Matthew 5 or what Paul said in Galatians 5 or what is proscribed for elders and deacons in 1 Timothy 3. Then read those prescriptions carefully and, after a clear interpretation, retrieve them for our day with minimal adjustments. A rough and ready originalism works along those lines.

But this is not how Jewish law worked, and any reading of church history will reveal that is not how New Testament instructions for followers of Jesus worked. (Nor does it adequately explain the history of American jurisprudence.) Law has origins, but law develops. To be sure, in a clear and compelling legal ruling—murder is wrong—adjustments might occur with punishments (capital sentence, fine, imprisonment) or in indirect, unintentional cases of causing death. In the development of law, one element comes to the fore in one case and in another case another element shapes a new ruling. Lamb for Passover: To boil or not? One book says cook only; another book of the law permits boiling. This is not careless choice of vocabulary by lazy authors but a law in development. Development of law is improvisation.[2]

The Ten Commandments prohibit work on the Sabbath. Fine, but on the second Sunday everyone began to ask, Is this work? Is that? And what about this situation? Some answers are worked out in the pages of the Hebrew Bible. Much more definition followed so that, by the time of Jesus, "work" had been nuanced in detail.[3] But Sabbath law development did not end in the first century. It still continues. A Sabbath day, indeed, remained, and remains for the observant, but precision required improvisation.

A sketch of the early phases of that development can begin in the instructions in Exodus where work is prohibited. But already before that law is found in the Decalogue the children of Israel were instructed to gather twice the volume of manna on the sixth day. Not working entailed not plowing, not making fires. An offering of required sacrifices on the Sabbath was permissible. In a new day more prohibitions were added, like not purchasing, and not treading grapes or gathering grain or transporting produce. Unintentional transgressions, Leviticus articulates, require a sacrifice. Intentional sins, like gathering of sticks on Sabbath, led to stoning in the wilderness journey to the land. Fighting a war on a Sabbath day, it was improvised, was not considered a violation of the prohibition of work.[4] Who knew?

A very clear law of Moses, taking a Sabbath day, required interpretation and adaptation and negotiation and improvisation, and this is how all law worked in Israel. By the time of the Mishnah these various Sabbath laws were put into a lengthy list of thirty-nine items that constituted work, but one cannot presume the well-known list in m. Shabbat 7:2 ends the negotiation.[5]

> A. *The generative categories of acts of labor*
> *[prohibited on the Sabbath] are forty less one:*
>
> B. *(1) he who sows, (2) ploughs, (3) reaps, (4)*
> *binds sheaves, (5) threshes, (6) winnows, (7)*
> *selects [fit from unfit produce or crops], (8)*
> *grinds, (9) sifts, (10) kneads, (11) bakes;*
>
> C. *(12) he who shears wool, (13) washes it,*
> *(14) beats it, (15) dyes it;*
>
> D. *(16) spins, (17) weaves,*
>
> E. *(18) makes two loops, (19) weaves two threads,*
> *(20) separates two threads;*
>
> F. *(21) ties, (22) unties,*
>
> G. *(23) sews two stitches, (24) tears in order to sew*
> *two stitches;*
>
> H. *(25) he who traps a deer, (26) slaughters it,*
> *(27) flays it, (28) salts it, (29) cures its hide,*
> *(30) scrapes it, and (31) cuts it up;*

    I. (32) he who writes two letters, (33) erases two
       letters in order to write two letters;
    J. (34) he who builds, (35) tears down;
    K. (36) he who puts out a fire, (37) kindles a fire;
    L. (38) he who hits with a hammer; (39) he
       who transports an object from one domain to
       another—
    M. lo, these are the forty generative acts of labor less
       one.

In addition to improvisations over time, we are not to assume there was only one singular and controlled set of developments. The rabbis of the Mishnah did not speak for all Jews of all time. Jesus's articulations of observance offered his alternative to how others observed the law, like the Sadducees, or the Qumran community, or the Zealots, or the Pharisees, who may well have had more than one formation by the time of Jesus. Each of these groups formed a praxis that articulated how to live faithfully in the covenant God had with Israel. In the world of Jesus each of these groups ramped up the significance of its own particular shape of observance. Intense polemics occurred.

Standing Jesus's something new with something more next to the other movements of his day permits a wider lens angle on how Christians are to live. In an informed and lively discussion of the "eye for an eye" saying in its various formulations in the Jewish world, we read that the "Pharisees [were] popular because their traditions . . . [quoting Josephus] 'alleviated the harsher prescriptions of the Bible in civil and criminal law.'" Words claiming the Pharisees were softer than their contemporaries always surprise most Christians because most think of the Pharisees as pettifogging fundies ready to pull out little Mishnahs hidden in their cloaks to quote chapter and verse. Ironically, the Pharisees were in some ways the progressives of their day because they routinely adjusted the law to current conditions. Hear this: compared with the Pharisees, Jesus was often the more stringent interpreter of the law. Their adaptations eventually led the rabbis, to take one example, to "build a fence around the death penalty," leading Judaism to go "out of its way to make execution, for any reason, impossible."[6] So, the law of Moses was not some rigid code. It was a flexible instrument in need of improvisation.

One short example from Jesus. In Mark 10:9 Jesus says this about God's design for marriage: "What God has joined together, let no one separate." His categorical words stun the disciples, probably because of the ease of divorce in the first century. Jesus then makes it a bit more explicit when he rules in legal form, "Whoever divorces his wife and marries another commits adultery against her; and if she divorces her husband and marries another, she commits adultery" (10:11–12). With a strong originalist assumption, one could say Jesus prohibits all divorce and all remarriage. Matthew's Gospel appears to improvise when he adds to the words of Mark's version. Matthew writes, "And I say to you, whoever divorces his wife,

except for unchastity, and marries another commits adultery"
(19:9, my italics). Matthew's addition confirms what the law
about divorce recorded in Deuteronomy 24:1–3, so perhaps
he's making more rigorous interpretation less rigorous. Paul,
however, improvises in a surprising manner in 1 Corinthians
7:12–16, which deserves to be quoted in full:

> *To the rest I say—I and not the Lord—that if any
> believer has a wife who is an unbeliever, and she
> consents to live with him, he should not divorce
> her. And if any woman has a husband who is an
> unbeliever, and he consents to live with her, she
> should not divorce him. For the unbelieving husband
> is made holy through his wife, and the unbelieving
> wife is made holy through her husband. Otherwise,
> your children would be unclean, but as it is, they are
> holy. But if the unbelieving partner separates, let it
> be so; in such a case the brother or sister is not bound.
> It is to peace that God has called you. Wife, for all
> you know, you might save your husband. Husband,
> for all you know, you might save your wife.*

It appears that the law of divorce, as interpreted by Jesus, was
originally quite rigorous. But it needed improvisation in at
least two cases within the space of a generation or two.

Today's conservative jurists, not least those persuasive to
America's fundamentalist Christians, are simply out of touch

with how the law was working in Jesus's world when they, to take another example closer to the topic of "humane" violence, vociferously defend the Bible's commands on capital punishment today with the interpretation that the "law is the law." They have become the very stereotype of the imagined "Pharisee" they have themselves inaccurately fashioned.[7] Debating the death penalty should not casually be relegated to a side show on America's stage. Sociologists can now correlate affirmation of the death penalty with Christian nationalism. The correlation tops out at 75 percent or so.[8] Read these lines:

> *The more that white Americans seek to*
> *institutionalize "Christian values" or the nation's*
> *Christian identity, the more strongly they support*
> *gun-toting good guys taking on (real or imagined)*
> *gun-toting bad guys, the more frequent use of the*
> *death penalty, any-means-necessary policing, and*
> *even torture as an interrogation technique.[9]*

Who Is Developing Law Now?

One authority's improvisation of a law created debates about improvisations by others.[10] It's clear that biblical laws "are not set in stone" and they "evolved over the centuries" and they are "demonstrably changeable" because the "Jewish tradition . . . has always had a character of a running argument." So a scholar asks about ongoing improvisation: "Is it not possible to envision further changes in light of vastly changed circumstances between the biblical period and our own time?" We cannot presume the Bible said all that was to be said about any legal or moral concern.[11] We who take our Bibles seriously will affirm the core commandments while knowing they will require timely improvisations.

The Bible's view of the Bible's own laws is that laws develop at the hands of God-honoring improvisers. But there's more to it than improvisation. What holds the Bible together is story, a story that shapes imagination and improvisation.

Story

History is a narrative created by the narrator, and not simply a record of what actually happened in the past. The conclusion that history takes shape as a narrative supplements the development of Jewish law as improvisation. One classic narrative approach to the Bible shapes the narrative in four moments: creation, then fall, then redemption, and finally consummation. But that narrative, embraced by a wide spectrum of the Christian church, *is only one* story of Israel. We have to ask now, "*Who* is telling the story?" We also now recognize that the one who tells the story controls the glory. The basic story varies with each author determining the plot, set of characters, problems, resolutions, and ultimate end. Deuteronomy, the prophets like Isaiah or Ezekiel or Daniel, Jesus when he spoke of "kingdom," the apostle Paul's story of mission to the gentiles, and the seer of Revelation's story—which wraps all of history and all of creation—vary considerably. They may each be captured by some ultimate metanarrative, the "story of every-thing," but the shape of the story told by each gives each narrative a different shape.[12] Who tells the story will be adjusted as well by Why that "Who" tells the story.

These various stories improvise on the basic elements of the story—God over all creation and Abraham and covenant and law and kings and prophets and Jesus and apostles and mission and the end of history. The improvised story develops in different ways in different settings.[13] Improvisation roots itself in the original script of Scripture as it innovates in our day in our way as Jesus and the apostles did in their way for their day.

Improvising always goes beyond the Bible[14] when it negotiates biblical texts with modern situations. Whatever we call these improvisations,[15] we are all improvising and we will continue to do so.

Integration

Improvisation as how to interpret the Bible for our day can disturb many Christians. But we must all admit that our theology impacts how we read the Bible and the Bible impacts our theology, and our context impacts both and everything in between.[16] None of us reads *just* the Bible and none of us articulates our theology *apart (or totally apart) from the Bible.* The Bible and articulations about the Bible tangle themselves into an integrated mass. Everyone who starts with the Bible goes beyond the Bible, and truth be told, no one actually starts only with the Bible. When an African American theologian announces up front that he reads the ethical orientations of the Gospels in order to foster liberation for African Americans, he is only admitting what each of us does.[17] We all operate beyond the Bible because the Bible cannot (always) be enough for our modern situations.

Even a former dean of evangelical scholars recognizes the reality of improvisation as the Bible's own way of mapping how Christians adapt and accommodate under changing circumstances:

> *What we have in the New Testament, therefore, is a combination of the apostolic deposit and Spirit-given insight. . . . The combination of a doctrinal, Christological criterion and a renewed mind enables believers to develop the implications of their faith and to come to fresh insights to deal with new knowledge and the danger of false belief. By these means believers were able to assess new revelations by prophets and new teaching of other kinds, and this led to a fuller development of doctrine.*

Notice the connection of "Spirit-given insight" to a "renewed mind," and a few pages later we read about "an incompleteness in Scripture" as well as "continuity throughout the process."[18] Improvisation has always been there and it will always be with us as we seek to embody a kingdom imagination today. Improvisation begins with Scripture as it probes new settings.

This is not the place to sketch the many approaches to an improvised peace ethic, though they are constant companions for those who want to develop a lived theology of a peaceful imagination.[19] A peaceful imagination has the power to stiff-arm and eradicate not only "humane" actions in war but all forms of violence, including the social, verbal, and physical violence of white Christian nationalism.

5

PEACEFUL IMAGINATION

AT SOME STOP in the journey into a peaceful imagination one learns that war robs what is God's—life and death—and transfers it into the hands of humans. A question that emerges in that journey is, How can a follower of Jesus put to death another follower of Jesus for the sake of a nation-state? That renders to Caesar what alone is God's. And, how can a follower of Jesus put a nonfollower of Jesus to death when it is the Christian's duty to offer Christ's redemption to them? To kill another human gives to Caesar what alone is God's.

At some level the dignity of humans revealed in the act of God in Christ renders war, which is designed to dominate by death, contradictory to the Christian gospel. Such a theological argument is compelling. Here is a confession of mine:

> *I cannot kill a non-Christian, for whom Christ has died and to whom I am called to preach the gospel, for the State; that would be rendering to Caesar what is God's and deconstruct the kingdom mission.*
>
> *I cannot kill a fellow Christian for the State; that would be rendering to Caesar what is God's. My first allegiance is to the king and to his kingdom people.*

> *I am called to cooperate with the State to the*
> *degree it is consistent with the kingdom; I cannot*
> *in good conscience cooperate with the State when it*
> *is inconsistent with the kingdom; that would be to*
> *render to Caesar what is God's.*
>
> *I cannot ask in the first instance if this is*
> *practicable. I am to ask in the first instance what it*
> *means to follow Jesus.[1]*

Following the teachings of Jesus is radical beyond calculation. These are some of the most important passages from Jesus that help us to form a peaceful imagination.[2]

Jesus's Creed of Love

Jews knew they were to love others because it was inscribed in their Scriptures. Jesus, when asked by a legal expert which one of God's 613 requirements was at the top of his list, made two central: love God and love others. Not by veering from the law of Moses but by a law-based hermeneutic of love. He combined, and in this he may have been the first to put them together in what could be called a creed-like manner, the Shema's love for God with a levitical demand to love one's neighbor as oneself (Deut 6:5–9; Lev 19:18). Again, love is a covenanted, affective committed relationship with another person that involves presence, advocacy, and mutual growth in virtue (a kingdom ethic for Jesus). The something more here is something "new" in becoming the ruling commandment.

It is impossible to embrace this something new, that is to love others, and to conduct war acts that lead, "humane" or not, to death. To love another person, to love another set of persons, to love persons in another nation, to love all persons—loving others will lead not to death but to peace and to justice. To war with others—real humans with real relations with real families in real nations—deals death. Death cannot produce peace through love but instead produces *Pax Romana*, which was really the subjugation of enemies through violent conquest or surrender. A specialist in the study of *Pax Romana* described it this way:

> *Precision is impossible, but we can confidently state that over the centuries millions died in the course of the wars fought by Rome, millions more were enslaved, and still more would live under Roman rule whether they liked it or not. The Romans were imperialists.*[3]

Jesus's peaceful imagination resists imperialism's grip and begins with a life shaped by love of God and others. The centrality of love in apostolic writings derives from what I have often called the "Jesus Creed" of loving God and loving others. Paul teaches the Romans that the commandment not to murder finds fulfillment in the command to love one's neighbor as oneself. To say it again but from a different angle, one cannot love others and put them to death in war when love forms into a covenanted, affective commitment to that same person or persons in a way that requires presence, advocacy, and mutual growth in virtue. Morally impossible.

The first foundation for a peaceful imagination grounds each of our behaviors and attitudes on loving God and loving others. Loving others turns radical in our next text to consider.

Love Your Enemies

Jesus eliminated war as an option for kingdom people. The most frequently cited text in the early church for defending Christian nonviolence is found at the end of Matthew's fifth chapter, where Jesus ordered his followers to love their enemies into neighbors.[4] One can't read the famous words about loving one's enemies, and not hear at least an echo of loving Rome.[5] Only by turning another human into one's enemy does one enter into war with that person. Jesus prohibits disciples from even having enemies.[6] If you have no enemies and make everyone into neighbors, there will be no war. The logic compels.

The occasion for Jesus's words must be guessed at, but probably someone thought loving one's neighbor or fellow Jews gives permission to "hate your enemy." By the time of Jesus, Jewish traditions moved in differing directions when it came to gentiles.[7] For some, gentiles were "others" or idolaters or unclean/inferior or even mostly to be avoided. But alongside this tradition, and probably almost always at the same time, gentiles were neighbors to be treated with civility and considered made in God's image. Of course, for some, gentiles became "enemies." Consider the so-called *Kittim*, probably Romans, of the Dead Sea Scrolls, from the opening column in the famous "War Scroll." (The war at hand would be between the Essenes of Qumran and the Kittim).[8]

> *On the day when the Kittim fall there shall be a*
> *battle and horrible carnage before the God of Israel,*
> *for it is a day appointed by Him from ancient times*
> *as a battle of annihilation for the Sons of Darkness.*
> *On that day the congregation of the gods and the*
> *Congregation of men shall engage one another,*
> *resulting in great carnage. The Sons of Light and*
> *the forces of Darkness shall fight together to show the*
> *strength of God with the roar of a great multitude*
> *and the shout of gods and men; a day of disaster.*

One cannot ponder these harsh words until one readily admits there's something profoundly, too profoundly, common about othering. America has a history of othering Native Americans and Mexicans. The United States others in its international relations, in its voting laws, in its racisms, and in its white Christian nationalism. What is characteristic of our country was characteristic of Romans, of Greeks, of Egyptians, and— let's be clear—of later imperial Christians from Constantine on. Othering leads to war. Loving the other (or enemy) unothers the other, and thus eliminates the possibility of war by improvising a peaceful imagination.

Jesus's something new of loving and praying for others transforms into neighbors the othering disposition of disregarding, discrediting, and degrading one's fellow human beings. The anchor for Jesus's peaceful imagination for enemies in the Sermon on the Mount is deeply lodged in the Creator's love for all humans (Matt 5:45). Jesus then ties this loving-the-other way of life to one piercing word: *perfect*. "Be perfect, therefore, as your heavenly Father is perfect." Let's just hope we're all right when we say Jesus didn't mean sinlessness! After all, he's Jewish; there's the temple, there's Yom Kippur, each of which displays profound awareness that all humans sin. No, Jesus means treating others the way the "heavenly Father" treats them, that is, by showering natural gifts on all, by loving all others.[9]

A peaceful imagination begins with loving others, but the imagination takes a long stride when Jesus calls his followers to love *enemies*. Turning an enemy into a neighbor makes it possible to enjoy the art of covenanted, affective love that requires presence, advocacy, and growth in virtue. Kingdom people do not war with neighbors. Kingdom people create neighborhoods.

Serve Others

The next statement by Jesus rivals in importance his well-known render-to-Caesar words. Jesus orders his disciples to behave opposite the Roman way of power and domination in Mark 10:35–45. James and John want the status and glory of sitting to the right and to the left of Jesus "in your glory." Jesus interrogates them, and playfully sets a trap. They have the temerity to think they can go through his baptism and drink his cup, only to be informed the baptism and cup are not what they think they are.

Instead of basking in the reflected glory of Jesus, he continues teaching them, they will have to choose between the way of Rome and the way of the cross. The way of Rome dominates others. Jesus offers a countercultural, counter-Rome way with an abrupt "not so among you." Instead, they are to serve one another and serve others. The something more of Jesus deconstructs and demolishes greatness, status, and glory 100 percent with a life shaped by serving others. Behind this something more is something new in leadership. The new image of leadership emerges out of the pattern of Jesus's own life. Jesus, the Son of Man, does not dominate with servants running around doing his bidding, but instead he arrives on the scene to "serve" and "to give his life a ransom for many."[10] The Son of Man saying of Jesus immediately morphs into a discipleship saying. Jesus, the one just confessed by Peter as Messiah, will be a crucified and resurrected Messiah. The ones who follow that kind of Messiah will be marked by the same kind of life, a life that takes its cues from the cross and suffering.[11]

A kingdom imagination. A peaceful imagination. Improvisation. Americans are wrestling one another to the ground in political and cultural wars. Christians do some of the tussling as well as cheering the wrestling match on. The peacemaker, however, searches for a way of loving and serving one's political "opponents" in order to make them neighbors. The peacemaker seeks common ground by listening to the other and learning from one another. The peacemaker considers how the other understands the other's point of view, and does not demonize the other. Even more, one cannot drop "humane" missiles and serve someone at the same time; one cannot torture another human and love them at the same time; one cannot hate someone and serve them at the same time. Improvisation, indeed. Rooted in kingdom and peace-loving imaginations.

The Only Tolerable Violence

A saying of Jesus appears in our Gospels in two versions, and because the Greek terms are needed to understand what has happened, they are put in brackets here:

> *From the days of John the Baptist until now the kingdom of heaven has suffered violence* [biazetai], *and the violent* [biastai] *take it by force* [harpazō]. *(Matt 11:12)*
>
> *The law and the prophets were in effect until John came; since then the good news of the kingdom of God is proclaimed* [euaggelizetai], *and everyone tries to enter it by force* [biazetai] *(Luke 16:16)[12]*

There is but one question here for the construction of a peaceful imagination: Is the violence a metaphor for something good or a description of something bad, namely, zealot-like force? One could read Matthew's "suffered violence" as a suffering text. Maybe John the Baptist is in the background. But Luke's version can't be read in a negative, suffering, violence-experiencing manner. More likely, we are to understand the violent images as irony. That is, they point at those now following Jesus with wholehearted passion, and the passion forms for Jesus into images sounding like violence. Thus, "the kingdom is indeed being 'taken by storm' [that is, followers are all-in] by the 'men of violence' [those willing to go all-in for Jesus's kingdom imagination]."[13] It is next to impossible to believe Jesus was exhorting his followers in some kind of first-century uprising to pick up arms and take Jerusalem by storm. This violent saying, then, is about the nonviolent practice of enemy love and utter commitment to the way of Jesus.

Rome's domination and physical violence are overruled by Jesus's version of violence, namely, by the kingdom's rule of love, enemy love, and a cross-shaped service.

Render to Caesar

No matter how many times we dunk the famous saying of Jesus about rendering to Caesar in a tub of water, it pops up each time with its resilient ambiguity. The question Jesus was asked seems to be a trap: "Is it lawful to pay taxes to the emperor, or not?" (Mark 12:14). Only Mark doubles it with

"Should we pay them, or should we not?" The question is clear. The answer is not, and maybe his answer is intentional "diplomatic ambiguity."[14]

Jesus recognizes the questioners' "hypocrisy" and knows they are testing him to get him into trouble with Jerusalem's authorities, who have to answer to Rome's authorities. If Jesus answers yes, he sides with the emperor and must answer to Jerusalem. If he answers no, he sides with Jerusalem and must answer to the emperor. Is he a rebel or not? That's the question. To answer their question Jesus asks for coin, a coin with an image of Tiberius on it. On that coin one would have read something blasphemous to (at least some of) Jerusalem's Torah observant. On the coin was written "son of the divine Augustus." The other side of the coin had an image of Roma, the goddess. Double jeopardy.

Which only slightly lessens the ambiguity. Jesus could mean that one should give back to Caesar what is Caesar's—this coin, taxes, pay them. What then is God's? Israel, the people of the covenant. Or, perhaps Jesus has split the world in half: the pro-culture side (Caesar) and the counterculture side (God, Jesus, and his kingdom). Any solution needs to fit the accusations against Jesus in his trial. Luke 23:2 informs an authority that Jesus has been caught "forbidding us to pay taxes to the emperor." If the accusation provides accurate information, Jesus's "what is God's" means *everything belongs to God*. Even the coin.[15] Remember, the issue at hand is whether or not Jesus was a rebel wannabe king. The entry into Jerusalem stoked some fires, and the temple incident tossed more fuel on that fire.[16] He is challenged about his (to them) absurd claims, so he challenges them in response.

He does not give his questioners all they want by answering them with a simple yes or no. He was averse to such responses. He offers instead suspense that drives them to decide. Jesus's all-consuming summons of a kingdom-fueled peaceful imagination summons to living before God with one's entire being. Including peacemaking. Instead of looking like a political rebel or anarchist, Jesus exemplifies peacemaking. The coin for him is an object lesson teaching that following him means one's entire life. Instead of being a rebel, he is the king who calls people—even his questioners—to do all they can to enter the kingdom, a kingdom established without violence by loving others and serving others.

The render-to-Caesar saying, then, is not a both/and but an either/or.[17] A peaceful imagination finds its way by turning life over to Jesus, a peaceful revolution that resists the way of Rome.

Imitate Jesus

Sometimes pastors and professors talk about how to live as Christians without thinking about what Jesus taught or how he himself actually conducted himself. Ignoring Jesus means not only missing out on his teachings about discipleship but also, and especially, ignoring that he called his followers to imitate his life.[18]

The human desire to imitate someone powerful can lead to the negative response inside a system sometimes called "mimetic desire," that is, a system of being driven by desire to compete and gain victory over a rival.[19] Mimetic desire, the desire to be great, is often unnoticed by those who affirm the role of imitation of Jesus. Imitating Jesus means resisting Rome's system of rivalry. But it means imitating one who instead of becoming a rival to others in the battles for victory, following Jesus sabotages rivalry itself. He sabotages the Roman system of mimetic rivalry by transforming his disciples *out of their desires for power into those who love others and serve others*. Jesus not only sabotages. He creates an alternative system of love and service and peace. Jesus calls people to a "*desire* to imitate the nonrivalrous, nonviolent Person."[20]

And nothing about the sickening craze in America's pseudo-claim to "humane" war is more certain than mimetic rivalry driving the competitions of the nations and its powermongering leaders into a war for domination. Conversely, nothing then can be more fruitful for a peaceful imagination than imitating Christ, because imitating Jesus, the servant who endured the cross, undermines corrupted mimetic desire.[21]

The fundamental cross and servant shape of a kingdom imagination and a kingdom discipleship reflects the contours of Jesus's own life. The apostle Paul's exhortations to his churches, while emphasizing life in the Spirit in fundamental ways, give more than a few clues that the Spirit-based life should look like the life of Jesus.[22] Paul says, "Be imitators of me, as I am of Christ" (1 Cor 11:1). To imitate Christ in Paul means to do everything for God's glory, to give no offense, and far more and especially "not seeking my own advantage, but that of many, so that they may be saved" (10:31–33). This sounds like the very teachings of Jesus we have already discussed. Imitation of Jesus will take the shape of Jesus's life. We see much the same in Paul's famous letter to the Romans.[23]

> *We do not live to ourselves, and we do not die to*
> *ourselves. If we live, we live to the Lord, and if we*
> *die, we die to the Lord; so then, whether we live or*
> *whether we die, we are the Lord's. For to this end*
> *Christ died and lived again, so that he might be*
> *Lord of both the dead and the living.*

There is tension in Rome between the weak and the strong, or the social profile of being powerless and powerful, with each convinced of one's view backed up with weaponizing Bible verses. Paul summons them away from their divisiveness to welcoming one another *by living out the pattern of Jesus's life.* Paul will then in the next chapter appeal to imitating Jesus in not pleasing oneself, in living in unity with one another, and in welcoming each other.[24]

Think, too, of the early Christian hymn quoted in Philippians' second chapter. At issue among the Philippians are "selfish ambition" and "conceit" and looking after one's own interests. The answer to self-aggrandizing behaviors of becoming great again is found in the pattern of Jesus's life, who "because he was God" or "though he was God," surrenders his status to enter into life with human slaves and to die on the cross and to be raised and to return to the Father's side with glory.

A Spirit-based life in Christ looks like Christ. A life that looks like Christ, as we have seen, turns away from violence and turns toward peacemaking because it has a kingdom imagination. At the heart of a peaceful imagination is the pattern of Jesus's own life. Imitating Jesus improvises peace. It perceives "humane" war as itself a crime. The something new with Jesus becomes an ongoing improvisation of something more for those who follow him.

Nonresistance or Nonviolent Resistance?

Matthew chapter 5's famous "do not resist an evildoer" seems like the tip of the top end of Jesus's utopianness as well as the depth of his impracticableness. The law at work in this famous saying of Jesus, the *lex talionis* or the law of justifiable retaliation, had less and less severe expressions of punishment as Jewish law developed: corporal equivalence, financial compensation, as well as (at times, but rarely) capital punishment.[25] One can easily get stuck on the law of Moses as a *requirement* for retaliation (or justice). One can read Deuteronomy that way. It reads, "Show no pity: life for life, eye for eye, tooth for tooth, hand for hand, foot for foot." "Show no pity" provides a categorical, unchangeable law should one want it to be that. So Jesus's overt prohibition of retaliation in "do not resist" seems to contradict Moses. But Jewish law did not turn Moses's law in this case into a rigid no-exception law. Jesus's prohibition may create some tension with statements from Moses. Perhaps Jesus thinks Moses was himself hyperbolic. Maybe Jesus was. Plus, we need to factor in developments in Jewish law, because its laws always led to fresh improvisations.[26]

Justice is the major topic at work behind Jesus's words. What kind of justice? Did he believe—to use our terms today—in rehabilitation or deterrence? Did he perhaps believe in retributivist or restorationist forms of justice?[27] It would be rash to force Jesus into our categories, but the words used of him in this particular passage clearly press against retribution and even deterrence, and urge upon the follower of Jesus to consider clarification, truth telling, repentance, forgiveness, and then to move toward rehabilitation, reparation, and restoration. Improvisation will determine which path one walks.

The gravity of Jesus's words always turns readers to consider the weight of these instructions: "Do not resist" and "turn the other cheek" and "give your cloak" and "give to everyone." These instructions lead their listeners or readers toward behaviors shaped by nonvengeance and nonviolence,[28] including, too, strong words denouncing injustices, foot-dragging annoyances, and acts of gracious enemy love that can shame the exploiting powerful into perceiving their violence. Jesus in this famous paragraph shames the exploiter and seeks to transform him into someone morally conscious of Rome's systemic exploitation. Resistance to Rome morphs into peacemaking in a nonviolent mode.

Jesus is not offering a utopian or impracticable ethic. He is radicalizing a kingdom imagination so that, by improvisation, it reaches into all of life, most especially here, and especially so here, in one's relation to political and economic exploiters. *Flip their script and see what happens*, that's his point. It takes a moral imagination, and daily improvisation, to walk with and behind Jesus.[29]

Peacemaking

A glance now at a sermon by Peter in the book of Acts. In the account of Peter's sermon we read this summary of the message of Jesus, a one-of-a-kind summary in the New Testament:

> *You know the message he sent to the people of Israel,*
> preaching peace by Jesus Christ—he is Lord of
> all. *(Acts 10:36, italics added)*

Peter's sermon summarizes Jesus's gospel message as one of *peace*. The sermon puts peace in the center of Peter's memory of Jesus's kingdom vision. Jesus's peace message leads Peter to mention Jesus's improvised acts of peace in benevolence and healing. A kingdom imagination improvises peace in many ways. This imagination comes from Jesus, and his example of what peaceful actions include can provide us with improvisations in our world. Peter summed up Jesus's message as peace because Jesus lived and preached peace.

In Luke's version of instructions for Jesus's agents of mission, we read this:

> *Whatever house you enter, first say, "Peace to this house!" And if anyone is there who shares in peace, your peace will rest on that person; but if not, it will return to you. (Luke 10:5–6)*

Matthew's version reads,

> *Whatever town or village you enter, find out who in it is worthy, and stay there until you leave. As you enter the house, greet it. If the house is worthy, let your peace come upon it; but if it is not worthy, let your peace return to you. (Matt 10:11–13)*

The NRSV has muted the Lukan words. Luke 10:6 can be rendered more literally as "if there be there a *son of peace*." The Matthean version has a greeting of peace, as does Luke. But the Lukan version enters into the home to find someone marked by peace. This saying also makes peace central to Jesus's kingdom imagination. The something new of Jesus (his kingdom vision) means something more, and peace beats in the heart of something more.

The Beatitudes of Jesus express divine favor and kingdom flourishing *for those who are otherwise deemed of no status.* That is, the Beatitudes bless *demographic people groups* who are marked by some virtue (like peacemaking). They are a kind of "who's in" and "who's not" list that must have turned his listeners upside down. These are the sorts of people who Jesus considers kingdom people.[30] On the seventh people group in Matthew's Gospel Jesus announces the favor of God for peacemakers. If we take a side glance at Luke's version of the Beatitudes we are not wrong in suggesting Jesus at least simultaneously implies a loud "Oy!" on the warmongering groups who think the way to God's kingdom comes by violence and bloodshed.

> *Blessed are the peacemakers, for they will be called*
> *children of God. (5:9)*

With the "Prophetic Imagination" chapter before this, and with a "Kingdom Imagination" added, we have plenty of information to define what peacemaking entails. To make peace, or to do peace, is to counter the way of violence and war and empire through God's reconciling work, Christ's pattern-shaping life, and the Spirit's empowering presence. A peaceful imagination resists all forms of violence and war as it pursues forgiveness, reconciliation, and unity among those near to and far from Christ. It means in Jesus's time resisting the way of Rome and the violent ways of the zealot types.[31] It means loving others, it means turning enemies into neighbors, and it means a life shaped by serving others and not dominating others.

It means in our time resisting the ways of empire and the violent ways of our "humane" acts of war. Peacemaking "consists of positive initiatives to overcome evil by employing *peaceable means* to make *peace*."[32] One cannot sublimate this peaceful imagination of Jesus into the world of private, personal relations. A person of peace does not pursue peace only in personal relations. In a person of peace a character of peace flourishes, and it moves from home into neighborhood and church and extends into community, state, and nation. Jesus's kingdom imagination cannot be reduced to personal religion because for him the kingdom is a community-shaped social reality.

Only peacemaking persons can be called "children of God" because, like God, they know the way of Jesus as the way of love, of a cross-shaped service, and of righteousness. These three mark the something more to which Jesus calls his followers, and they are radically incompatible with all the ways of war, "humane" or not. As Jesus said it, "My kingdom is not *from* here" (John 18:36), but it is God's kingdom come *to* here.

* * * * * *

On the day I was editing this book I was pointed to a webpage called The Christendom Curriculum. Here is its opening paragraph:

> *Welcome to* The Christendom Curriculum,
> *America's only* **Christian Nationalist homeschool**
> **curriculum.** *You've just found the homeschool*

> *option that's not only easy to use, and the lowest price*
> *for the best value, it's also the only one that prepares*
> *your children for the reality of Culture War—with a*
> *view toward long-term victory.*[33]

The next paragraph reveals its opponents:

> The Christendom Curriculum *offers your children*
> **a strong education in the Bible and the Great**
> **Books of Western Civilization,** *completely* **free of**
> **Woke ideology.** *You'll have the comfort of knowing*
> *your children are growing in knowledge and wisdom*
> *without having your family's values undermined*
> *by teachers or textbooks compromised with Leftist/*
> *Globalist/Social Justice propaganda.*

What was once an uncomfortable label ("Christian nationalist") has become not only acceptable but something about which one can be proud. The aim of this curriculum prepares children for the culture wars. Its claim of a biblical education defies the central themes of a kingdom's peaceful imagination. Daily on my Twitter feed I see more and more of this form of American Christian nationalism. It mocks the peaceful imagination of Jesus.

A peaceful imagination inspired by a kingdom imagination that takes its cues from the life of Jesus challenges every breath taken on webpages like the one above. Its idolatrous commitment to America as a Christian nation, its agenda against everything progressive, equates God and Christianity and America with one side of the aisle, and its conflation of Bible with America borders on the idolatrous. Racism, idolatry, and violence seep into the fabric of Christian nationalism. It is the opposite of what Jesus teaches in his kingdom vision in loving one another, loving one's enemies, and serving others in order to form a larger neighborhood.

The three elements of Jesus's peaceful imagination— love of God and others, love of enemies, and serving others— form the foundation for improvisation in our world today. We dare not turn the words of Jesus or the Bible into what they never were: rigid codes that refuse adaptation in new contexts. The core elements of Jesus's kingdom imagination require that the follower of Jesus improvise. We can improvise in our home in the formation of children and as we love one another into virtuous kingdom character. We can improvise in our neighborhoods by learning about one another and serving one another. We can improvise in our churches in formation, in service to one another, and in serving our communities in consort with others who embody the kingdom imagination of Jesus.

One person at a time.

One day at a time.

One neighborhood at a time.

One community at a time.

And, God willing, one nation at a time.

We can walk in a lived kingdom imagination when we refuse to permit churches to wage wars of self-promotion in the hypocrisies of self-protection, when we demand from our pastors that they be marked by character and refuse to become personas on a platform who preach sermons in order to promote numbers instead of discipleship in a peaceful imagination. We live out a peaceful imagination as followers of Jesus by walking in peace with one another, by loving one another, by loving those with whom we differ, and by picking up the towel and basin of service instead of the sword of power and domination.

In learning in home and church the formation of kingdom's peaceful imagination we can extend that formation into the public—in local communities, in states, in our nation, and in our global community. We do this constructively by supporting policies and politicians who care about love of God and others, love of enemies, and serving one another. We can do this resistantly and dissidently when we gain lenses to perceive the presence of Babylon in our communities, states, and nations. When we see injustices and war and recognize the rhetoric of "humane" attached to war actions, when we take note of policies that foster death and torture, when we perceive politicians using rhetoric that bristles with lies in order to protect a party, when we recognize racisms and economic injustices, and when we are awakened to history books that do not tell the truth about American history and silence the voices of our own oppressed and marginalized. When we become dissidents of violence and war and death and the blasphemies of "humane" acts of war and the idolatries of "white, Christian" nationalism.

A peaceful imagination is not a preference, nor is it a political option. It's the way of Jesus. Go and do improvisation.

NOTES

1. Poverty of Imagination

1 Philip S. Gorski and Samuel L. Perry, *The Flag and the Cross: White Christian Nationalism and the Threat to American Democracy* (New York: Oxford University Press, 2022), 84.

2 Samuel Moyn, *Humane: How the United States Abandoned Peace and Reinvented War* (New York: Farrar, Straus and Giroux, 2021). I quote from pp. 4, 5, 6, 10.

3 Mohammad Yunus Yawar, Idrees Ali, and Jeff Mason, "U.S. Kills al Qaeda Leader Zawahiri in Kabul Drone Missile Strike," Reuters, August 2, 2022, https://www.reuters.com/world/cia-carried-out-drone-strike-afghanistan-us-officials-say-2022-08-01/.

4 Antony J. Blinken, Secretary of State, "The Death of Ayman al-Zawahiri," U.S. Department of State, August 1, 2022, https://www.state.gov/the-death-of-ayman-al-zawahiri/.

5 Gorski and Perry, *Flag and the Cross*, 95–96. On a second insurrection, 103–30.

6 John Rodden, *Becoming George Orwell: Life and Letters, Legend and Legacy* (Princeton, NJ: Princeton University Press, 2020).

7 *Agricola* 3.30 AT.

8   Nigel Biggar, *In Defence of War: Christian Realism and Just Force* (Oxford: Oxford University Press, 2013).

9   Robin W. Lovin, *Christian Realism and the New Realities* (New York: Cambridge University Press, 2008).

10 See Rom 16:20; Acts 10:36; Eph 6:15; Rom 5:1; 14:19; Gal 1:3; 1 Cor 7:15; Eph 2:14–18; Col 1:19–20. On peace, see especially Willard M. Swartley, *Covenant of Peace: The Missing Peace in New Testament Theology and Ethics* (Grand Rapids: Eerdmans, 2006); Richard B. Hays, *The Moral Vision of the New Testament: Community, Cross, New Creation: A Contemporary Introduction to New Testament Ethics* (San Francisco: HarperOne, 1996).

11 Moyn, *Humane*, 37.

12 Moyn, *Humane*, 306.

13 Moyn, *Humane*, 309.

14 Scot McKnight, "Jesus, Bonhoeffer, and Christoform Hermeneutics," appendix 3 in *Discipleship in a World Full of Nazis: Recovering the True Legacy of Dietrich Bonhoeffer*, by Mark Thiessen Nation (Eugene, OR: Cascade, 2022), 193–213.

15 The focus here will only be on war, but one can think too of power and capital punishment with our justice system and its blindness to restorative and distributive justice. On which see Martin Hengel, *Christ and Power*, trans. Everett R. Kalin (Philadelphia: Fortress, 1977); Christopher D. Marshall, *Beyond Retribution: A New Testament Vision for Justice, Crime, and Punishment* (Grand Rapids: Eerdmans, 2001).

16 Among the many who have said this, see Ronald J. Sider, *Nonviolent Action: What Christian Ethics Demands but Most Christians Have Never Really Tried* (Grand Rapids: Brazos, 2015); David C. Cramer and Myles Werntz,

A Field Guide to Christian Nonviolence: Key Thinkers, Activists, and Movements for the Gospel of Peace (Grand Rapids: Baker Academic, 2022).

17 By "violence" I refer to killing but also to psychological and physical damaging of another person.

2. Prophetic Imagination

1 See Perry B. Yoder, *Shalom: The Bible's Word for Salvation, Justice, and Peace* (Eugene, OR: Wipf & Stock, 2017); Swartley, *Covenant of Peace*.

2 On imagination, see esp. Ruth M. J. Byrne, *The Rational Imagination: How People Create Alternatives to Reality* (Cambridge, MA: Bradford, 2005).

3 All translations are from the NRSV unless otherwise designated Goldingay, Alter, or AT (author's translation). John Goldingay, *The First Testament: A New Translation* (Downers Grove, IL: IVP, 2018); Robert Alter, *The Hebrew Bible: A Translation with Commentary* (New York: W. W. Norton, 2018).

4 Swartley, *Covenant of Peace*, 27–52. The quotation comes from 27.

5 Isa 2:4; Mic 4:3; cf. Joel 3:10. What follows is from Isa 9:6–7 and 32:17–18.

6 The following citations, in order, are from Isa 51:11; 52:7–8; 54:2, 3 (Goldingay), 10, 13 (Goldingay); 55:12; 60:17; 66:12–14; 14:13; 33:9; Jer 29:7; Ezek 34:25; 37:26; Zech 8:12, 16–17; Ps 122:6–8.

7 Matt 5:9; 10:34; Luke 10:4–6; 19:42.

8 John 14:27; 16:33; 20:21, 26.

9 An older book but still of much value is Martin Hengel, *The Zealots: Investigations into the Jewish Freedom*

Movement in the Period from Herod I until 70 AD, trans. David Smith (Edinburgh: T&T Clark, 1997). The story of Masada has been challenged. See Steve Mason, *A History of the Jewish War: AD 66–74* (Cambridge: Cambridge University Press, 2019); Jodi Magness, *Masada: From Jewish Revolt to Modern Myth* (Princeton, NJ: Princeton University Press, 2019).

10 In this paragraph: Rom 14:17; 15:33; 16:20; Eph 2:14, 17; 4:3; 6:15.

3. Kingdom Imagination

1 Ronald J. Sider, *If Jesus Is Lord: Loving Our Enemies in an Age of Violence* (Grand Rapids: Baker Academic, 2019).

2 Matt 1–2; 3:3; 4:1–16; 8:16–17; 9:13; 10:34–36; 11:10; 12:16–21, etc.

3 Dale C. Allison Jr. and W. D. Davies, *A Critical and Exegetical Commentary on the Gospel According to Saint Matthew*, vol. 1, International Critical Commentary (Edinburgh: T&T Clark, 2000), 59.

4 Matt 11:12 and Luke 16:16.

5 No verb is used, which means the verb is underdetermined and the NRSV's "were in effect," however reasonable, is overdetermined.

6 The view I take here can be found in Joel Marcus, *Mark 1–7*, AB 27 (New York: Doubleday, 2000), 245–46.

7 Mark 14:12–31.

8 Scot McKnight, *Jesus and His Death: Historiography, the Historical Jesus, and Atonement Theory* (Waco, TX: Baylor University Press, 2005), 243–334.

9 John 6:52–58.

10 James D. G. Dunn, "John 6: A Eucharistic Discourse?," *NTS* 17 (1971): 328–38.

11 Scot McKnight, "Covenant and Spirit: The Origins of the New Covenant Hermeneutic," in *The Holy Spirit and Christian Origins: Essays in Honor of James D.G. Dunn*, ed. G. N. Stanton, Bruce W. Longenecker, and Stephen Barton (Grand Rapids: Eerdmans, 2004), 41–54.

12 James D. G. Dunn, *The Acts of the Apostles* (Grand Rapids: Eerdmans, 2016), 12. Italics mine.

13 See Gal 3:19–29.

14 2 Cor 5:17.

15 1 John 2:7–8.

16 Important discussions of the 1980s and 1990s include Marcus J. Borg, *Jesus: A New Vision: Spirit, Culture, and the Life of Discipleship* (San Francisco: HarperSanFrancisco, 1991); John Dominic Crossan, *The Historical Jesus: The Life of a Mediterranean Jewish Peasant* (San Francisco: HarperCollins, 1992); N. T. Wright, *Jesus and the Victory of God*, Christian Origins and the Question of God 2 (Minneapolis: Fortress, 1996); Paula Fredriksen, *Jesus of Nazareth, King of the Jews: A Jewish Life and the Emergence of Christianity* (New York: A. A. Knopf, 1999).

17 At the same time as Fredriksen I mapped the discussion of inaugurated eschatology in Scot McKnight, *A New Vision for Israel: The Teachings of Jesus in National Context* (Grand Rapids: Eerdmans, 1999), 70–155. I draw from those pages in the next paragraphs.

18 Mark 1:14–15; Matt 11:25–27; 13:16–17.

19 Mark 2:19; 4:11; Luke 4:16–30.

20　Mark 4:30–32; Luke 7:21–23; 11:20; Mark 3:27.

21　Mark 1:16–20; Matt 7:21.

22　Mark 10:45.

23　Matt. 10:23; Mark 9:1; 13:30; Luke 22:28–30; Matt 16:19.

24　Luke 13:34–35; 19:41–44; 22:28–30; Mark 13; Matt 20:20–23; 25:31–46.

25　Luke 12:32; Matt 13:43; 25:34; 26:29.

26　Developed in Scot McKnight, *Kingdom Conspiracy: Returning to the Radical Mission of the Local Church* (Grand Rapids: Brazos, 2014).

27　A word seemingly deleted in almost all translations is "greatly" (*pleion*), an adverb that intensifies the verb "exceeds" (*perisseuō*).

28　The best discussion of righteousness is still Benno Przybylski, *Righteousness in Matthew and His World of Thought*, SNTSMS 41 (Cambridge: Cambridge University Press, 1981).

29　References in this paragraph: John 13:34–35; 1 John 2:7–8; Mark 12:23–34 par. Matt 22:34–40; Luke 10:25–28; Deut 6:1–9; Lev 19:18; cf. Matt 19:19.

30　Swartley, *Covenant of Peace*. That he can write more than five hundred pages in anything but breezy prose about peace in the NT unmasks those who have ignored it (names omitted).

31　The "evildoer" of Matt 5:39 and the "enemy" of 5:43 may be referring to those pointed at in 5:11, 22, and 25; on which see esp. Dorothy Jean Weaver, "Transforming Nonresistance: From *Lex Talionis* to 'Do Not Resist the Evil One,'" in *The Love of Enemy and Nonretaliation in the New Testament* (Louisville, KY: Westminster John Knox, 1992), 32–71.

32 Amy-Jill Levine, *Short Stories by Jesus: The Enigmatic Parables of a Controversial Rabbi* (New York: HarperOne, 2015), 77–115.

33 Scot McKnight, *Pastor Paul: Nurturing a Culture of Christoformity in the Church*, Theological Explorations for the Church Catholic (Grand Rapids: Brazos, 2019), 41–48. See also John Goldingay, *Old Testament Theology: Israel's Gospel* (Downers Grove, IL: IVP Academic, 2015), 332–43; Jon D. Levenson, *The Love of God: Divine Gift, Human Gratitude, and Mutual Faithfulness in Judaism* (Princeton, NJ: Princeton University Press, 2016); Saul M. Olyan, *Friendship in the Hebrew Bible*, ABRL (New Haven, CT: Yale University Press, 2017).

34 See Drew Strait, "Peace, Reconciliation," in *Dictionary of Paul and His Letters*, 2nd ed., ed. Scot McKnight, Lynn Cohick, and Nijay Gupta (Downers Grove, IL: IVP Academic, 2023), forthcoming.

35 Deirdre J. Good, *Jesus the Meek King* (Harrisburg, PA: Trinity Press International, 1999), 1.

36 Richard A. Burridge, *What Are the Gospels?: A Comparison with Graeco-Roman Biography*, 3rd ed. (Waco, TX: Baylor University Press, 2020).

37 Who better to point this out than Richard A. Burridge, *Imitating Jesus: An Inclusive Approach to New Testament Ethics* (Grand Rapids: Eerdmans, 2007).

38 Jack Dean Kingsbury, "The Verb AKOLOUTHEIN ('To Follow') as an Index of Matthew's View of His Community," *JBL* 97 (1978): 56–73. My emphasis here comes with the term "community with the suffering."

39 Notice Phil 2:6–11; Col 1:15–20.

40 Michael J. Gorman, *Cruciformity: Paul's Narrative Spirituality of the Cross*, new ed. (Grand Rapids: Eerdmans, 2020); McKnight, *Pastor Paul*.

4. Improvisational Imagination

1 For a good example of how his theory works out see Scalia's writings in Antonin Scalia and Ruth Bader Ginsburg, *Scalia Speaks: Reflections on Law, Faith, and Life Well Lived*, ed. Christopher J. Scalia and Edward Whelan (New York: Crown Forum, 2017).

2 Exod 12:8–9; Deut 16:5–7. Michael Fishbane, *Biblical Interpretation in Ancient Israel* (Oxford: Clarendon Press, 1985), 134–36.

3 Exod 20:8–11; 16:4–5, 22–23; 34:21; 35:3; Num 28:9; Neh 10:31–32; 13:15–22; Jer 17:19–27.

4 Lev 4:27–31; Num 15:32–36; 1 Macc 2:29–41.

5 Translation from Jacob Neusner, *The Mishnah: A New Translation* (New Haven, CT: Yale University Press, 1988).

6 Amy-Jill Levine and Marc Zvi Brettler, *The Bible with and without Jesus: How Jews and Christians Read the Same Stories Differently* (New York: HarperOne, 2020), 184, 190.

7 See the exceptional collection of essays in Joseph Sievers and Amy-Jill Levine, eds., *The Pharisees* (Grand Rapids: Eerdmans, 2021).

8 Gorski and Perry, *Flag and the Cross*, 95.

9 Gorski and Perry, *Flag and the Cross*, 95–96.

10 John J. Collins, *The Invention of Judaism: Torah and Jewish Identity from Deuteronomy to Paul* (Berkeley: University of California Press, 2017).

11 John J. Collins, *What Are Biblical Values? What the Bible Says on Key Ethical Issues* (New Haven, CT: Yale University Press, 2019), 12, 13.

12 On both the various narratives in play and the story of everything, see James D. G. Dunn, *Jesus Remembered*, Christianity in the Making 1 (Grand Rapids: Eerdmans, 2003), 387–406; McKnight, *Kingdom Conspiracy*, 43–63; C. Kavin Rowe, *Christianity's Surprise: A Sure and Certain Hope* (Nashville: Abingdon Press, 2020).

13 Samuel Wells, *Improvisation: The Drama of Christian Ethics* (Grand Rapids: Baker Academic, 2018); Kevin J. Vanhoozer, *The Drama of Doctrine: A Canonical-Linguistic Approach to Christian Theology* (Louisville, KY: Westminster John Knox, 2005).

14 I. Howard Marshall, *Beyond the Bible: Moving from Scripture to Theology* (Grand Rapids: Baker Academic, 2004).

15 "Socio pragmatics" for Anthony C. Thiselton, *New Horizons in Hermeneutics* (Grand Rapids: Zondervan, 1992), 379–470. "Associative hermeneutics" for Love Lazarus Sechrest, *Race and Rhyme: Rereading the New Testament* (Grand Rapids: Eerdmans, 2022), 1–44.

16 Scot McKnight, *Five Things Biblical Scholars Wish Theologians Knew* (Downers Grove, IL: IVP Academic, 2021); Hans Boersma, *Five Things Theologians Wish Biblical Scholars Knew* (Downers Grove, IL: IVP Academic, 2021).

17 Brian K. Blount, *Then the Whisper Put on Flesh: New Testament Ethics in an African American Context* (Nashville: Abingdon, 2001).

18 Marshall, *Beyond the Bible*, 71, 78. In Marshall's book Kevin Vanhoozer has a valuable response, mostly affirm-

ing but nuancing the "Marshall Plan" (81–95), and Stanley Porter insightfully connects Marshall to the dynamics in translation theory (97–127).

19 Cramer and Werntz, *A Field Guide to Christian Nonviolence*; William J. Webb and Gordon K. Oeste, *Bloody, Brutal, and Barbaric? Wrestling with Troubling War Texts* (Downers Grove, IL: IVP Academic, 2019); John Dominic Crossan, *Render unto Caesar: The Struggle over Christ and Culture in the New Testament* (San Francisco: HarperOne, 2022); Claude F. Mariottini, *Divine Violence and the Character of God* (Eugene, OR: Wipf & Stock, 2022).

5. Peaceful Imagination

1 Scot McKnight, *The Sermon on the Mount*, Story of God Bible Commentary (Grand Rapids: Zondervan, 2013), 132.

2 I write about my journey in Scot McKnight, *The Audacity of Peace*, vol. 14, My Theology (Minneapolis: Fortress, 2022).

3 Adrian Goldsworthy, *Pax Romana: War, Peace and Conquest in the Roman World* (New Haven, CT: Yale University Press, 2017), 11; see also Mary Beard, *S.P.Q.R.: A History of Ancient Rome* (New York: Liveright, 2016).

4 Ronald J. Sider, ed., *The Early Church on Killing: A Comprehensive Sourcebook on War, Abortion, and Capital Punishment* (Grand Rapids: Baker Academic, 2012). See also George Kalantzis, *Caesar and the Lamb: Early Christian Attitudes on War and Military Service* (Eugene, OR: Cascade, 2012).

5 Notice the Roman echoes, too, in Matt 5:38–42.

6 Levine and Brettler, *The Bible with and without Jesus*, 197–200.

7 On which see G. Gilbert, "Gentiles, Jewish Attitudes Toward," in *The Eerdmans Dictionary of Early Judaism*, ed. John J. Collins and Daniel C. Harlow (Grand Rapids: Eerdmans, 2010), 670–73.

8 Gen 10; 17:20; 1 Sam 8:5, 20; Deut 12:30; 1 Kgs 11:1–4; Isa 44; Josephus, *Jewish War* 1.152, 354; cf. Deut 7 to Ezra 9; Philo, *Life of Moses* 1:23–24; Josephus, *Antiquities* 2:412–416; Sirach 36:11–17; *Sibylline Oracles* 5:493–500; 1QM 1:9–11.

9 For a sketch of the meaning of "perfection," see esp. Ulrich Luz, *Matthew 1–7*, rev. ed., Hermeneia (Minneapolis: Fortress, 2007), 290–91.

10 See McKnight, *Jesus and His Death*, 159–75.

11 Cf. Mark 8:34–9:1; 9:33–37; 10:35–45; also Swartley, *Covenant of Peace*, 92–120.

12 It is next to impossible to determine which of these is the more original, though some have tried. See Paul Hoffmann, John S. Kloppenborg, and James M. Robinson, eds., *The Critical Edition of Q*, Hermeneia (Minneapolis: Fortress, 2000), 464–67.

13 Dunn, *Jesus Remembered*, 452–53. See also Wright, *Jesus and the Victory of God*, 468–69.

14 Dunn, *Jesus Remembered*, 650.

15 Remember too that the word at work here is "image" (*eikon*), and the image of God pertains to humans made in God's image. God's created *eikons* are called to image God in this world. Caesar's image on that coin is not the same as God's image on all humans.

16 This saying may well be a countercultural response to the Maccabean line of violent rebellion and resistance:

"Pay back the Gentiles in full, and obey the commands of the law" (1 Macc 2:68).

17 Wright, *Jesus and the Victory of God*, 502–7, esp. 504.

18 Burridge, *Imitating Jesus*.

19 René Girard, *The Scapegoat*, trans. Yvonne Freccero (Baltimore: Johns Hopkins University Press, 1989).

20 Swartley, *Covenant of Peace*, 357.

21 Swartley, *Covenant of Peace*, 375.

22 Jason B. Hood, *Imitating God in Christ: Recapturing a Biblical Pattern* (Downers Grove, IL: IVP Academic, 2013).

23 Quoting Rom 14:7–9, but notice also 15:3, 5, 7.

24 Scot McKnight, *Reading Romans Backwards: A Gospel of Peace in the Midst of Empire* (Waco, TX: Baylor University Press, 2019), 27–33.

25 In this paragraph we quote or allude to Matt 5:38–42; Num 35:31; *m.B.Q.* 8:1; Deut 19:21; Judg 1:6; Lev 19:18; Prov 20:22; 24:29 as well as Jub 4:31–32; Josephus, *Ant.* 4.280; Philo, *Spec.Leg.* 3.182, 195, 197; *m. B.Q.* 8:1; *b. B.Q.* 83b–84a.

26 Levine and Brettler, *The Bible with and without Jesus,* 186–200. The previous references are from 212–15. For a broad sketch of the law of the talion, see William Ian Miller, *Eye for an Eye* (Cambridge: Cambridge University Press, 2005).

27 For a solid study, see Marshall, *Beyond Retribution*, 97–143, 145–99.

28 Some have argued that "do not resist" (*anthistēmi*) owes its natural sense in military resistance. One good example is Walter Wink, "Neither Passivity nor Violence: Jesus' Third Way (Matt. 5:38–42 par.)," in *The Love of Enemy and Nonretaliation in the New Testament*, ed.

Willard M. Swartley (Louisville, KY: Westminster John Knox, 1992), 102–25, esp. 113–16.

29 I take the expression from Dale C. Allison, *The Sermon on the Mount: Inspiring the Moral Imagination* (New York: Herder & Herder, 1999).

30 One sees a similar listing in Sirach 14:20–27; 25:7–11.

31 Martin Hengel, *Victory over Violence*, trans. D. E. Green (London: S.P.C.K., 1975); Hengel, *Christ and Power*.

32 Swartley, *Covenant of Peace*, 46.

33 https://www.christendomcurriculum.com/. All emphases are theirs.